Speak

to the

Mountain

God Can Make You Well

Christine Darg

EVANGELISTA MEDIA™ srl
Via Maiella, 1
66020 San Giovanni Teatino (Ch) – Italy

"Changing the World, One Book at a Time."

This book and all other Evangelista Media™ and Destiny Image™ Europe books are available at Christian bookstores and distributors worldwide.

To order products, or for any other correspondence:

EVANGELISTA MEDIA™ srl
Via Maiella, 1
66020 San Giovanni Teatino (Ch) – Italy
Tel. +39 085 959806 • Fax: +39 085 9090113
Email: info@evangelistamedia.com

Or reach us on the Internet: www.evangelistamedia.com

ISBN 13: 978-88-6880-055-0
ISBN 13 EBOOK: 978-88-6880-050-5

Second Edition (First Edition of 2,000 published in the Holy Land.)

For Worldwide Distribution, Printed in the U.S.A.

2 3 4 5 6 / 17 16 15 14

DEDICATION

To Jesus, who paid (in Jerusalem) the terrible price for our healing with many sacred stripes from the Roman scourges!

To Jerusalem: "Nevertheless, the time will come when I will heal Jerusalem's wounds and give it prosperity and true peace" (Jer. 33:6 NLT).

To Israel: "For I will restore health unto thee, and I will heal thee of thy wounds, saith [YHVH]; because they called thee an Outcast, saying, This is Zion, whom no man seeketh after" (Jer. 30:17).

To every seeker of the Lord, our Healer: May you find His healing balm in these pages!

ACKNOWLEDGMENTS

Thanks to my publisher, Pastor Pietro Evangelista, for your encouragement and dedicated effort to distribute my books far and wide.

Thanks also to editor Donna Scuderi for your excellent "Points to Ponder" at the end of each chapter.

And loving thanks to my husband Peter who always strengthens me with "like precious faith" (2 Pet. 1:1).

ENDORSEMENTS

Christine Darg says what my spirit has known for years. When you get the healing and Israel connection right, healing will flow!

Sid Roth
Host of "It's Supernatural!"

Christine Darg is one of the few twenty-first century evangelists who is able to write with authority on the subject of divine healing. I have been privileged to witness firsthand the miracles that have confirmed Christine's ministry. This book reveals the heart of one who is totally committed to the 'full gospel,' including the healing of the sick. Christine is truly a gift to the Church, and her ministry is a blessing to all the people and nations to whom she is called to minister.

Dr. Tony Stone
International Speaker and Chairman of Exploits Ministry

At Revelation TV, we have been privileged to show Christine Darg's program, "Exploits," for many years. Christine is a woman of faith unafraid to proclaim the Word of God where many others fear to tread! The message contained in *Speak to the Mountain* is one proven in Christine's own life and confirmed in the lives of many with whom she has prayed. I commend Christine to you, and pray that you and many others will take up the challenge put forth in this book.

Gordon Pettie
Chairman, Revelation Foundation

CONTENTS

FOREWORD

My father, W.G. Hathaway, raised me with a simple childlike faith in the truth of God's Word. He was born again as a young man, in the days of the Welsh Revival, and became a pioneer of Britain's early Pentecostal Movement, working with healing evangelist George Jeffreys.

In *Speak to the Mountain,* Christine Darg expresses her simple, practical faith—the kind we need to see God's promises fulfilled in our lives. Fifty years ago, I had throat cancer. By faith, I stood on God's Word and was totally healed! Then, just ten years ago, lung cancer struck. Once again, I placed my faith in God and His Word. In three months' time the cancer came out of my body, *without any medical treatment!*

It is the Spirit of God and the Word of God together that will revolutionize your life. The Bible teaches that "God is not a man, that He should lie" (Num. 23:19 NKJV). What He says, He does; whatever He has spoken, He will make it happen!

I encourage you to do what Christine says in this book. Speak to the mountains in your life with the power and authority of the Word of God, and the Spirit of God will bring it to pass! Seek this kind of faith—not as a hearer only, but as one who receives His Word and puts it into practice.

Rev. Dr. David Hathaway
Evangelist

Introduction

Just as repentance and forgiveness of sins must be preached from Jerusalem, Jesus also commissioned His disciples to heal the sick. Salvation of the soul without the healing of the body proclaims a half-truth, an amputated Gospel.

The same Holy Bible that says, "For God so loved the world that he gave his only Son, that whoever believes in him should not perish but have eternal life" (John 3:16 RSV), also freely offers us Matthew 8:17: "...Himself took our infirmities, and bare our sicknesses."

There is no beatitude in the Bible for being sick. Concerning healing, the tenor of Scripture is summed up in Third John 1:2: "Beloved, I wish above all things that thou mayest prosper and be in health, even as thy soul prospereth." Often, upon healing someone, the Lord would say, "Go in peace" (see Mark 5:34; Luke 7:50; 8:48). In the Old Testament, the Hebrew word for this peace is *shalom,* which means "untroubled, undisturbed well-being, wholeness." What a good definition of health!

If the Law goes forth from Zion and the word of the Lord from Jerusalem, that word includes healing, for it was here in the City of the Great King that the Healer made atonement for our bodies and souls. And it is to Jerusalem that He will return, with healing in His wings!

There is a connection between loving and praying for the peace of Jerusalem, and our physical well-being: "Pray for the peace of Jerusalem: they shall *prosper* that *love* thee" (Ps. 122:6). When we love Jerusalem and crave her peace, we commune with God's heart intimately, and therefore His many graces flow abundantly to us. We are not strangers to the Lord when we comprehend His jealous love for Jerusalem and His people. Wellness springs from our inner being outward. Surely the chief blessings of prosperity in this lifetime are that our sins have been forgiven and our sicknesses healed.

We encourage people to come on pilgrimage with us to the City of the Great King! We have seen many people healed in Jerusalem. Some have received creative miracles during our tours in the streets, on the ramparts of the Old City walls, and in our "Tabernacle of David" meetings. Jerusalem, in fact, is my "hospital." When I breathe the atmosphere of the "city of our God…the joy of the whole earth" (Ps. 48:2), I am at once consoled, restored, and even rejuvenated!

During one of our New Year prayer walks on the ramparts of the Old City walls, a deaconess from London received two brand-new kneecaps! She was scheduled for surgery and was walking with two canes. By faith she decided to go on the ramparts walk without the aid of the two sticks because she sincerely believed that the Lord Himself had hidden them. She testified that she could not find the two sticks in her hotel room, and when she finished our prayer walk on the walls, her knees were totally restored! That night the deaconess danced the *hora* in our convention, and joyously fell down on her new knees at the altar to give glory to the risen Healer!

A woman on one of our prayer walks was healed of heart disease. Another was healed of a debilitating bladder ailment. An Israeli woman who walked on crutches and resorted to a wheelchair was healed after she released forgiveness to the Palestinians who had tortured her son, a soldier in the Israeli Army. A Palestinian who was organizing a Gospel outreach for us was healed instantly of a tumor (which burst and vanished after prayer), and his scheduled operation was cancelled. A Muslim-background believer was healed of several major life-threatening attacks on his health after prayer.

On the Via Dolorosa, the Way of Sorrows, our Lord received manifold stripes on His body so that, by His wounds, we are healed of every disease and infirmity. The Lord's work of atonement is a permanent memorial in Jerusalem and permeates the atmosphere. His Shekinah Presence is palpable, and in First Kings 9:3 the Lord promised that His eyes and heart would always be here. In the soon–coming Millennium, Jerusalem will be called *Yehovah Shammah,* meaning, "The Lord Is There" (see Ezek. 48:35).

Truly, He *is* here! I sense the Lord's presence in Jerusalem more than any other place, because this city is the dwelling place of God. It *is* His residence, the City of the Great King!

Many of the messages in this book have been preached for many years, in various meetings during the Feast of Tabernacles. The meetings occurred at Israel's National Convention Center and were organized by the International Christian Embassy Jerusalem. Other messages were given during a monthly series of services at Christ Church, Jaffa Gate, and in our own Exploits Ministry's open-air meetings at Nafoura Old City Walls Restaurant. In addition, they were shared in open-air meetings on the Mount of Olives and at the American Colony Hotel in East Jerusalem, where our ministry was previously headquartered.

It is my ardent prayer that every reader will find lasting help in these pages and proclaim with me the words of Psalms 118:17: "I shall not die, but live, and declare the works of the LORD!"

Christine Darg
Jaffa Gate, Jerusalem

Chapter 1

TALK TO MOUNTAINS!

...Have faith in God. For verily I say unto you, That whosoever shall say unto this mountain, Be thou removed, and be thou cast into the sea; and shall not doubt in his heart, but shall believe that those things which he saith shall come to pass; he shall have whatsoever he saith (Mark 11:22-23).

Talking to mountains is not "normal" behavior in this world, but it *should* be normal activity for believers. Jesus tells us to talk to mountains! He wants us to command obstacles to move and walls to fall. His instruction in God's Word is His guarantee that God will honor our faith *if* we will believe and have no doubt in our hearts.

But when Jesus says you have to believe, you do have to *believe*. When? You have to believe when you speak your prayer (not later). And there really must not be any doubt in your heart.

We have to train ourselves to begin to recognize doubt and then reject it. Martin Luther used to say that no man was wicked because unclean birds lit upon his head; but if he allowed the birds to build their nests in his hair—*that* was wicked.

God works with and responds to *words*. No wonder Jesus taught His disciples to *talk* to big heaps of trouble. Speaking to mountains is an almost unbelievable concept. It does not seem logical, yet the Lord instructed us to do it. Can we accept His ways?

Speaking Enforces the Promise

God created our bodies to live forever. The entrance of sin in the Garden of Eden changed that; however, the Good News of the Gospel tells us that Jesus redeemed us from the curse and consequences of sin! Although the wages of sin is still death (see Rom. 6:23), we have many exceedingly precious Bible promises of divine health. These promises stand until the day we die (or until we arise in the Rapture).

Many times we think we are suffering degenerative diseases simply because we are getting older. Regardless of what we think, we can have the gift of health in old age. Healing and health are among the Gospel benefits we will study in this book. We must learn how to speak Bible promises and the truth of God's Word concerning the health that Jesus died for us to receive. That is why we must learn the concept of speaking to mountains.

I can imagine Jesus sighing to Himself and thinking, "Believers complain to Me about their problems, but I want them to talk to their problems!" Jesus instructed us to command the mountain to be thrown into the depths of the sea, where it would disappear from sight. If, for example, you are suffering with pain or cancer, say aloud to the symptoms, "Pain! Cancer! I'm talking to you! Wither and die from the roots up! Leave my body!"

Strange as it may seem and sound, that is what the Lord told His disciples to do. His *modus operandi* is: "Don't tell Me about your mountains. Tell your mountains about Me!" Instead, most of us pick up the telephone, or send a text message, or email our most spiritual friends to ask for prayer. But according to Jesus, exceptional faith talks directly to the mountain!

Believing the Unchanging God

If you are sick, the Good News is that Jesus has never changed (see Heb. 13:8). Despite human cynicism concerning healing, He refuses to change. Scripture makes clear: "I am the LORD, I change not..." (Mal. 3:6).

One of the ways God never changes is that He is a rewarder. Although salvation is the free gift of God, He does reward faith. Hebrews 11:6 declares: "But without faith it is impossible to please him...he is a rewarder of them that diligently seek him." *Rewarder* means "one who pays wages."[1]

Who fulfills the requirement of Hebrews 11:6 today? When you hear the conversations of most whining, whimpy, miserable "believers," you have to admit that most Christians are "unbelieving believers." They live in the lowlands of faith, constantly confessing doubts, uncertainties, worry, complaints, and negative statements about their health, bodies, families, and work. The Bible labels the lack of faith as sin! Romans 14:23 declares that "whatever is not from faith is sin" (NKJV). Ouch! We must swallow that "Gos-pill!" Furthermore, Hebrews 3:12 warns us: "Take heed, brethren, lest there be in any of you an evil heart of unbelief, in departing from the living God."

On the other hand, if you keep talking to your mountain and do not entertain doubt in your heart, Jesus guarantees that the mountain will disappear! Do you believe Him?

On the way back from Bethany, Jesus spoke to a fig tree. He cursed the tree, and it withered from the roots and died (see Mark 11:12-14; 20-21). When will we learn that our words are powerful?

Know His Will

A friend who was married to a healing evangelist was in hospital with cancer. Even after being married to a man of faith for nearly fifty years, she still had not comprehended the healing message! She prayed with uncertainty, saying, "If it be Thy will...," rather than saying to the mountain, "Cancer, leave my body!"

There is a proper time to pray "If it be Thy will." James 4:13-15 explains: "...ye that say, To day or to morrow we will go into such a city, and continue there a year, and buy and sell, and get gain: whereas ye know not what shall be on the morrow....For that ye ought to say, If the Lord will, we shall live and do this, or that."

When we are uncertain of God's will concerning a journey, a house move, job change, marriage partner, and so forth, we should say, "If it be God's will."

However, where healing is concerned, God's Word makes His will very clear: "Is any sick among you? let him call for the elders of the church; and let them pray over him, anointing him with oil in the name of the Lord: and the prayer of faith shall save the sick, and the Lord shall raise him up…" (James 5:14-15).

In the Greek, *let him call for* means to "summon."[2] The verb is in the imperative tense, which demands immediate action. This Scripture is a direct command that every sick believer should at once call for anointing prayer. Notice what this passage does *not* say. It does not say, "The prayer of faith shall save the sick, if it be God's will." Or, "The Lord shall raise him up, if it be His will." So why do we add to the Word of God?

Stand, Speak, Overcome

God promises to heal us, but He does not always tell us when the healing will manifest. Sometimes He tests our faith. The passing of time can become a stumbling block, causing us to miss God through impatience and unbelief. So many of us give up and stop believing God after a single hour or day. But can we believe Him for a week? A month? A year? A decade? When our faith fully pleases God, the healing manifests.

Walking in divine health requires training. God trains us to be overcomers. He wants strong overcomers to rule with Him. And we have to train ourselves to speak to mountains. We have to be reprogrammed by the Holy Spirit.

Since it is not "normal behavior," you must learn to speak out loud to the obstacle. The first time you speak to a mountain by faith, it is unlikely that you will hear the sound of faith in your voice. Faith has a sound, and you will begin to recognize it as you walk with God. As you faithfully continue speaking to your situation, your spirit will hear, and your spirit and body will strengthen and begin to respond to your voice. Faith will arise and healing will follow. The key is to practice the ways of God until His ways become operational and second nature in your spirit.

We must open our mouths and speak, commanding the opposing mountain of sickness to be removed! We must emulate God our Father who calls things into existence as though they already exist (see Rom. 4:17). That is what Abraham, the father of faith, did; he believed God before his circumstances worked out favorably.

Not only do we *command* healing to come but we must also command sickness to *leave*. We certainly do not deny our symptoms; but symptoms are not our focus. We are to relax and realize that healing is a process. Miracles happen instantly, but healing is a recovery process. Do not throw away your medications; but as your faith grows and becomes stronger, you will discover that you need less medication. Eventually, your healing will manifest.

God truly wants you to be healed. He is ready to heal you, but He wants you to receive Him as Healer. Put your healing future into His care. He is your Physician. Build your faith in His Word. You will never regret it!

The Lord has been my Savior since childhood. He has graciously healed me and saved my life on a number of occasions. I saw the Lord in an open vision when I was a toddler, and He healed me, intervening miraculously to save my young life. But I did not fully and consciously (as an act of my will and my faith) receive Him as Healer until I was in my thirties.

And what a blessing it has been!

Tips on Talking

Talking to oneself is often equated with being crazy or senile, but it is part of speaking to mountains! God's ways are not our ways (see Isa. 55:8). He tells us to speak out loud to the problem.

A fascinating truth from the Gospels involves the woman with the issue of blood. She kept speaking to herself, saying inwardly, "If I can touch even the hem of Yeshua's garment, I shall be healed!" (See Matthew 9:21.) She received what she believed, and she demonstrated the power of speaking faith to oneself!

David in the Old Testament also encouraged himself in the Lord (see 1 Sam. 30:6). Nobody else was going to do it for him. No doubt, David understood that faith is confidence in God and is produced by words in our mouths.

Remember that God has a real appreciation for faith and takes note of those who speak their trust in Him! We are to follow the example of Jesus, who instructed us to speak to the mountain and to use words to demonstrate the power of God! It is so important to watch what we say! The Bible warns that every idle word will be judged (see Matt. 12:36). We are learning that God honors faith talk and judges unfaithful speech! Just as talking to mountains is of paramount importance, so are occasions of silence! One of the greatest Bible principles we must learn is that God hates grumbling and complaining. He will allow us to be inflicted with sickness because of sins of speech and His immutable laws of sowing and reaping (see Gal. 6:7-8).

Penalties are demanded by God's justice for sin and rebellion. Jesus paid the penalty for us, but our disobedience can compromise the immunity from sickness and disease already purchased by Him. Even if Satan is permitted to test us with sickness (as in the case of Job in the Bible), it is the nature of God to heal and to restore.

Always guard very carefully what you say about your body and your health in general. (Actually, it is not even wise to joke about getting old, becoming decrepit, catching the flu, etc., because your spirit hears and your body follows what you repeatedly or even carelessly say.)

Here is an example: In a healing service, a man was gloriously delivered from epilepsy and enjoyed his healing for many years. He no longer needed to take the more than twenty medications prescribed for him, and did not suffer a seizure for years. Then he backslid into sin, which I believe resulted in a road accident. He found himself waking up inside a hospital.

A doctor said, "According to your medical history, I see that you have seizures." "Yes," the man answered. He became careless with his words, adding, "I have epilepsy." Immediately his body obeyed his words and he suffered a seizure on the spot! How did this relapse happen after he had been healed for so many years? The Bible teaches in

Proverbs 18:21 that "Death and life are in the power of the tongue: and they that love it shall eat the fruit thereof." A modern translation would be, "They shall eat their words." Therefore our words had better be choice and good to eat!

"I didn't mean to say to the doctor, 'I have epilepsy,'" said the man. However, the Bible does not say you shall have what you mean; it says in Mark 11:23 that you shall have what you say! The man had suffered no seizures for years until he confessed having them.

The man repented, and his healing was restored.

Speak Life Only

So, is what you say important? Yes! Extremely important! God has decreed that "Death and life are in the power of the tongue..." (Prov. 18:21). Notice that because of our fallen condition, death is mentioned before life in this verse. Our tongues can either speak death (our fallen nature), or we can be reprogrammed through the regeneration of our spirits to speak *life!* Unfortunately, some of the ways that we speak death include careless, thoughtless words; negative words of destruction; cruel and mocking words; dangerous flattery or slander; lies and indecent talk. Our tongues can just as easily be instruments of life. Either way, our words clearly advertise whether we are diseased or healthy. The content of our conversations reveals the true state of our hearts and minds.

I was having coffee with a friend who asked me to pray for "her" disease. I said, "I would like to pray *against* the disease and command it to leave in Jesus' name, but you are choosing to own it. You call it *your* disease as though it belonged to you."

During ministry time in our meetings, people in the healing lines often say to me, "Please pray for *my* diabetes," or "my cancer," or some other ailment. As long as they own the disease as their special possession, why should it leave? For some people, disease has a perverted kind of pride attached to it. Don't give place to this! Train your spirit to rise up in a holy anger against sickness or infirmity and say, "Be gone from me! You are not mine. I do not own you. You are trespassing in my body. Leave me *now* in the name of Jesus!"

The Lesson of Miriam

Our mouths have more power over our destinies than we realize! There is a powerful exhortation in Ecclesiastes chapter 5. The warning is found in the context of making vows:

> *Suffer not thy mouth to cause thy flesh to sin...wherefore should God be angry at thy voice, and destroy the work of thine hands?* (Ecclesiastes 5:6)

Just as God heard Miriam and Aaron murmuring against their brother Moses, He can also become angry at the sound of our voices making wrong, arrogant, hurtful, or inaccurate utterances! When we hear inappropriate words proceeding from our mouths, we must train ourselves to cancel those words quickly. Negate them, in Jesus' name!

God has been trying to get us to learn this lesson almost from the beginning. The prophetess Miriam was a prime biblical example of one whose mouth called down guilt upon her own flesh. She was a righteous woman, a leader, and indeed a prophetess. As a young girl, Miriam was courageously willing to risk her own life for the sake of her baby brother, Moses. Their mother had hidden Moses in a basket on the Nile River so that he might escape the execution carried out against male Hebrew babies. Miriam acted as his faithful guardian, hiding in the bulrushes until he was brought to safety by Pharaoh's daughter.

But after Israel's exodus from Egypt, on the way to the Promised Land, Miriam gossiped, drawing her brother Aaron into the plot. Together, they spoke evil words against the man of God, Moses, and his wife. Moses nobly bore the insults and apparently did nothing to defend himself, but the Bible says that God heard what was said. You can be sure that God listens, weighs spirits, and vindicates His servants. According to the account in Numbers 12, the three siblings were summoned before the Lord, and the two murmurers were rebuked. As the main offender, Miriam suffered the disgrace of leprosy for her sin. For seven days, she was banished from the camp as someone unclean. Miriam was totally humiliated because of her presumptuous words. Only after Moses prayed to God for her, was she healed.

When we are tempted to gossip and to speak against God's man or God's woman, I can guarantee you that the best preventative medicine is silence. One great rabbi said, "All my days I have been raised among the Sages, and I have found nothing better for oneself than silence...."[3] Unfortunately, most people today are uneducated in the ways of God. Ignorant of what God hates, they do not make mental preparations to set a guard over their lips. And so they are likely to utter the first words that pop into their minds without any forethought or concern about how their words might be hurtful or might result in guilt.

The Torah demands that the people of God remember how the Lord humbled Miriam because of her words. She was made an example so that we will learn not to slip up through slander! As was true of Job's detractors (see Job 42:7-10), Miriam was healed only after intercession from the brother she had wronged. God protects His faithful servants who are maligned. Many people do not realize that their illnesses are a consequence of their uncontrolled and bitter tongue-lashings against servants of the Lord.

Do not do it! Do not do it! Learn to avoid slander literally like the plague! And especially do not speak against the Lord's ministers. It is simply not worth it, and can result in sickness. "We are commanded to make known the episode of Miriam to our offspring and to relate this episode to future generations," noted Nachmanides, the famous Jewish commentator and healer. "It would have been proper to conceal this embarrassing episode to cover as it were the disgrace of an otherwise righteous woman. Nevertheless, Scripture commands that we make it known and revealed, so that we be well versed in the prohibition of forbidden speech, which is a great sin and brings about many bad happenings, yet it's so frequently transgressed among the people of God."[4]

Forbidden Speech and Acceptable Words

Concerning forbidden speech and what the rabbis call the *lashon hara,* the evil tongue, it is wise to meditate upon Psalms 19:14 if we want to remain healthy: "Let the words of my mouth, and the meditation of my heart, be acceptable in thy sight, O LORD, my strength, and my redeemer." "The tongue of the wise brings healing," according to

Proverbs 12:18 (NASB). The famous Hasidic rabbi Breslover Rabbi Nachman (1772-1810) was not known to be a follower of Jesus (only God knows, of course). Nevertheless, he taught some of the same biblical principles about the power of words.

Nachman recommended to his disciples the pouring out of one's soul before God and talking to God on a daily basis as to a best friend or to a father, in one's own native tongue. The Rebbe instructed his leading disciple that when praying profusely in seclusion, he should "speak at length to each and every limb of his body, explaining to them that all bodily cravings are empty pleasures, for everyone ultimately dies, the body decomposes in the grave and all the limbs will rot."[5]

After following this advice for some time, the disciple lamented to the Rebbe that his body was completely deaf and insensitive to his arguments and words. But the Rebbe answered that perseverance was needed: "Be strong in this and don't waver. Eventually you will see what has come from these words....One also must tell oneself many words of encouragement so that one not give up entirely."[6] Amen! The same idea is found in First Samuel 30:6, where "David encouraged [strengthened] himself in the LORD his God."

Unwavering Faith Moves Mountains

In all that we say and do, we have to learn to act in faith. When we pray for others to be blessed or healed, we must not say or think, "Well, I hope God is listening." Equally wishy-washy is, "Let's pray and try God."

Do you hear any faith in those statements? No! We must pray *decisively* at all times. The prayer of faith is forceful and does not waver! Pastor Thurman Scrivner, a former Baptist deacon who has a worldwide healing ministry, prays decisively for people; and after they have repented from their sins, he says, "I *guarantee* you that God has healed you!"

People ask, "How can you guarantee healing?"

Pastor Thurman answers, "My statement is based upon the fact that I believe God's Word is true and that God cannot lie. If we believe what He has promised in the Bible concerning healing, we will pray decisively and without wavering and guarantee results based upon His Word!"

Speaking to mountains applies in all areas of faith, not just healing. In the tenth century, Cairo's Mokattam Mountain was literally moved by faith. This saved Christians from persecution after the Caliph challenged Coptic Christians to fulfill Matthew 17:20 (Jesus' promise about mountain-moving faith).

The Caliph said they must prove the words of Jesus or die! A Coptic saint named Simon the Tanner gave the faith command after believers fasted for three days, and the mountain that was obstructing the Caliph's view jumped three kilometers! Onlookers glimpsed the rising sun under the mountain as it jumped.

The monastery of Saint Simon commemorates the miracle which occurred at the time of the 62nd Coptic pope named Abram. God led us to visit that historic mountain; and at that place, He instructed us to speak to the mountain of religious opposition. He did not tell us to shout, to sing, or to pray; He told us to speak to the mountain of spiritual opposition to be moved.

We did exactly as we were told. Obstacles were removed. The Lord opened for our ministry an extraordinary door to set up a Gospel tent not far from the Mokattam Mountain in one of the greatest citadels of the Arab world.

Speak to mountains. It works! It is first-class faith! Speaking powerfully is one of the ways that we human beings were created in the image of God:

> *By the word of the LORD were the heavens made, their starry host by the breath of his mouth....For he spoke, and it came to be; he commanded, and it stood firm* (Psalms 33:6,9 NIV).

Points to Ponder

1. How do human concepts of what is "normal" oppose the image of God within us?

2. Explain the connection between knowing God's will and walking in faith.

3. "Death and life are in the power of the tongue: and they that love it shall eat the fruit thereof" (Prov. 18:21). How have these words become more meaningful to you since reading this chapter?

Notes

1. "Greek Lexicon: G3406 (KJV)," *Blue Letter Bible,* http://www.blueletterbible.org/lang/lexicon/lexicon.cf m?Strongs=G3406&t=KJV (accessed October 21, 2013).

2. Biblesoft's New Exhaustive Strong's Numbers and Concordance with Expanded Greek-Hebrew Dictionary, CD-ROM, Biblesoft, Inc. and International Bible Translators, Inc. (1994, 2003, 2006) s.v. "proskaleomai," (NT 4341).

3. Shimon ben Rabban Gamliel, Ethics of the Fathers, 117, from "Inspirational Quotes," beliefnet.com, http://www.beliefnet.com/Quotes/Judaism/S/Shimon-Ben-Rabban-Gamliel-Ethics-Of-The-Fathers-117/All-My-Days-I-Have-Been-Raised-Among-The-Sages-An.aspx?q=Study (accessed October 26, 2013).

4. Israel Meir, *Chofetz Chaim, A Lesson a Day: The Concepts and Laws of Proper Speech Arranged for Daily Study* (New York: Mesorah Publications, 2005), 137.

5. Rabbi Nachman, *The Outpouring and Revival of the Soul* (Rabbi Israel Dov Odesser Foundation, 2009).

6. Ibid.

Chapter 2

First-Class Faith

Speaking to mountains is first-class faith. Believing God for your healing is also first-class faith. Others may preach a weak Gospel, but true believers proclaim the full power of God and believe Him at all times—not just at church, but at home on a daily basis! The Good News that Jesus paid the price for our salvation *and* our healing is an indivisible Gospel; salvation and healing are inseparable.

Just as repentance and forgiveness of sins must be preached from Jerusalem, Jesus also commissioned His disciples to heal the sick. It bears repeating: to proclaim the salvation of the soul without the healing of the body is a half-truth, an amputated Gospel.

What is God's attitude toward sickness and disease? In the Bible, both God and Jesus hate disease; but somehow our modern view of sickness is muddled. The ambivalence of most persons toward God and His promises resembles the rhyme, "He loves me, he loves me not."

Many are taught to pray for healing with the same uncertainty, saying, "If it be God's will." Yet an Evangelical would never pray that way for salvation from sin. Evangelicals believe salvation is for anybody who chooses to receive Jesus. But the Church at large has not fully embraced and comprehended the idea that the Lord's salvation *includes* the healing of our bodies.

Until you are convinced that God wants you well, you will always experience doubt about whether you can be healed. Before you can exercise faith for healing, you must dissolve doubt.

Be a Dissolver of Doubt

Daniel was described as possessing "an excellent spirit, and knowledge, and understanding, interpreting of dreams, and shewing of hard sentences, and dissolving of doubts…" (Daniel 5:12). In the Hebrew, this verse literally means that Daniel had ability in "untying knots." In other words, he could answer knotty, intricate, and difficult questions.

I hope this book will dissolve any doubts about the healing aspect of the Good News. These doubts exist because the truth has become entangled and confused; but the confusion need not continue. God's will for your healing is fully stated in the Word. The Lord's wonderful Word and power will save and heal anybody! You can command any demon to leave your body, in Jesus' name. If you have made Jesus your Lord and Savior, it does not matter what your religious or ethnic background is. Anyone who dares to trust Yeshua the Messiah can be eternally saved, healed, and delivered.

But it doesn't happen by chance! The blessings of God belong to His obedient children and to those who will believe His "exceeding great and precious promises: that by these ye might be partakers of the divine nature…" (2 Pet. 1:4).

Contending or Complaining?

We must aggressively contend for the faith once delivered to us, the saints (see Jude 1:3). But most people are not contending. Instead, they are complaining. Is it any wonder that chronic complainers have a long medical history? God sent snakes to bite His people in the wilderness because they were grumblers and complainers.

Professing Christians are also capitulating to doubt today. In denominational churches, most Christians do not have a vibrant revelation of the Healer, and certainly most believers are still on the fence with a big question mark in their minds concerning God's will for divine healing.

The Healing Mindset

Healing is the most convincing demonstration of Emmanuel, God With Us! We must appropriate the healing gifts of the Lord and overcome any prejudices we might harbor against the healing ministry because of certain excesses or foibles of various healing ministers. The unchanging Gospel message is clear: "These signs shall follow them that believe; in my name…they shall lay hands on the sick, and they shall recover" (Mark 16:17-18).

Jesus never once suggested to a blind, deaf, crippled, or infirm person to coexist with a disease or infirmity to the glory of God. He never commanded anybody to bear a disease as a cross in order to follow Him. When He said that His follower should "take up his cross, and follow me" (Mark 8:34), the Lord was speaking of hardships and persecutions, but He never once called sickness a cross. Nowhere in the Bible does Jesus encourage a sick person to accept with finality a life marked by disease. On the contrary, in the Gospels we continually discover Jesus attacking sickness, disease, and infirmities as the works of Satan, which He came to destroy! This should be our mindset, too.

So, how far did Yeshua go with healing? Did He heal amputees? Yes! Matthew chapter 15 records that He healed not only the lame, but also the maimed. *Maimed* here refers to a "crippling injury, especially a loss of a limb." The Message version puts it this way:

> *They came, tons of them, bringing along the paraplegic, the blind, the maimed, the mute—all sorts of people in need—and more or less threw them down at Jesus' feet to see what he would do with them. He healed them. When the people saw the mutes speaking, the maimed healthy* [i.e., restored], *the paraplegics walking around, the blind looking around, they were astonished and let everyone know that God was blazingly alive among them* (Matthew 15:30-31 MSG).

And He's blazingly alive today! Say "Amen"! He is alive, but we are in a spiritual war zone in this earth. If you do not talk to mountains, resist the devil, and stand on God's promises, God may allow you to die prematurely. God does not love you any less, but there is a price of faith, and activity required to maintain divine health. Casual inquirers in prayer usually do not win health battles.

First-class, wonder-working faith, on the other hand, is speaking to mountains, commanding disease to depart in Jesus' name, and continuing to stand steadfastly on the Word, giving no place to the devil.

Healing is not a "game" of chance like the lottery! We pay the price by building our faith. In Luke 22:31-32, Jesus spoke to Peter (and to all disciples in the tunnel of time), saying: "Satan has demanded…to sift you like wheat; but I have prayed for you, that your faith may not fail…" (NASB).

Healing On Credit

I believe God often heals us because our faith did not fail! He will heal because of what we say or do, unless, of course, we are healed on somebody else's faith!

Healing that comes because of your faith is truly first-class faith. Healing resulting from somebody else's faith is not exactly first-class faith. It is, however, better than nothing! Reaping the benefit of somebody else's anointing and strong faith can be likened to being healed "on credit." Credit cards are fun and convenient because they offer instant gratification, but there's an obvious downside: you eventually have to produce the goods! And if the credit card bill is not paid on time, heavy penalties in the form of interest are exacted.

In my opinion, it is the same with divine healing. You can be healed on the faith and anointing of somebody else who has paid the price with God; but to stay well, you must eventually produce your own faith. Even if you have been saying the wrong things and thinking negative thoughts, Jesus will often heal you "on credit" because of His compassion and mercy (or because of His response to a faith person's command). But sooner or later the Creditor must be paid. You have to come up with the "cash," and in this analogy, faith is the currency.

To maintain your healing, you must develop your own unwavering faith. Can you see that? Your adversary the devil at some point will challenge your healing or your general health with a symptom, and then what will you do? Panic? Waiver? Cave in? Or, will you rise up and resist the devil? Will you believe and maintain your healing while Satan flees with his symptoms?

Healing Is Gospel!

Who of us would deny that with God all things are possible? Therefore I boldly say it is possible for any deformed person, any sick child, any blind person to be healed.

However, you do not get saved or healed by coincidence. God does not save people by chance, and He does not heal people by accident. He responds to acts of faith and to the prayer of faith (see James 5:15). God saves people when they repent and ask to be saved by believing and putting their trust in the Savior, Jesus the Messiah. Likewise, God heals people who repent and ask for healing in Jesus' name.

A spontaneous gift of faith is sometimes granted from the Lord as the Holy Spirit wills. However, normally faith does not grow as a gift. Faith does not materialize by accident, but it comes by hearing the Word of God (see Rom. 10:17). Faith increases because you feed your God-given measure of faith with the vitamins of God's Word. You decide to believe, to decree, and to obey Scripture regardless of what you see, feel, and hear. God's power then honors your faith and gives you victory. "Thou shalt also decree a thing, and it shall be established unto thee: and the light shall shine upon thy ways" (Job 22:28).

Indeed, healing is central to the doctrine of Messiah. Every time you meet Jesus in the Bible, He has just healed someone or is on the way to heal someone. I was deeply impacted when I heard Reinhard Bonnke say, "Healing is not an accessory to the Gospel." Yet doubters like to "unscrew" healing from the Gospel as if it were an accessory. First-class faith doesn't see healing as an add-on; it believes that healing is an integral part and parcel of the Good News. Early Christians regarded healing as the ordinary response of a loving heavenly Father to His children. Today in many Christian circles, the attitude has changed drastically. Modern churches err by teaching that sickness is a cross to carry. But welcoming sickness as a friend is a radical shift from the biblical view of sickness as an enemy! In Mark 1:41, when the leper asked Jesus if He was willing to heal, Jesus graciously answered, "I am willing!" In He-brew, the verse is rendered, "Ani rotze," meaning, "I want to!"

In the Gospels, sickness is treated as an enemy. The New Testament norm is to petition the Lord for relief from sickness and suffering. There-fore we must steadfastly resist embracing sickness as a friend. First-class faith makes no pact to coexist with sickness, disease, and infirmities.

To deny the healing power of Messiah is to deny the Gospel. In Isaiah 53:4, the record concerning the Lamb of God is this: "Surely he hath borne our griefs [Hebrew: sicknesses],[1] and carried our sorrows [Hebrew: pains]."[2] What a Savior! Jesus suffered every category of wounds, external and internal, and by His all-encompassing wounds we were/are healed! (See Isaiah 53:4–5 and First Peter 2:24.)

The apostle Peter summarized the ministry of Jesus: "…God anointed Jesus of Nazareth with the Holy Ghost and with power: who went about doing good, and healing all that were oppressed of the devil; for God was with him. And we are witnesses of all [these] things…" (Acts 10:37-39). Jesus' followers are supposed to duplicate and multiply His ministry! We must be diligent in this. If we do not stay on top of the healing message, we can lose it or become dull. Like everything else, we have to keep ex-ercising, meditating on, and eating the Lord's Word to maintain first-class faith. "Iron sharpens iron" (Prov. 27:17). Therefore, I recommend listening regularly to excellent healing teachers to help maintain first-class faith.

The doubt and unbelief in this world will dilute, overpower, and even destroy faith if we are not diligent. Many healing teachings are continu-ously available on the Internet (including our own at www.exploits.tv). These resources can sharpen your faith twenty-four hours a day, seven days a week. I listen most evenings to an excellent healing teacher to keep my spirit sharpened by his faith.

Power over Darkness

No doubt you have witnessed the following: One person always ap-pears to be in trouble; nothing seems to go right for him, and he dies at an early age. Another person seems always to hear from God and to re-ceive blessings, including divine health. What is the difference?

Blessings and curses are a reality. When I had a newspaper career in my twenties, I worked with another woman reporter who was heavily involved in the occult. She was fascinated by astrology and fortune-tellers. She was perpetually sick, a miserable person with aches and pains, childless, and always in trouble with the boss. Yet she could never receive correction about her fascination with the occult. She refused to see that she was bringing God's disfavor upon her life by trafficking in the occult. Someone with first-class faith would have been open to correction and would have recognized that the Bible speaks of blessings *and* curses.

The average churchgoer seems to talk as if chains or habits and sins are unbreakable. But Satan himself is the weakest link in chains of sin and sickness, because his chains are forged upon lies! God has equipped all believers to overcome Satan's power. The apostle Paul said that "the weapons of our warfare are not carnal [of a fleshly or earthly nature] but mighty through God for pulling down strongholds..." (2 Cor. 10:4 NKJV).

First-class faith resists and renounces the powers of darkness. If you or any of your ancestors have delved into the occult, these unhealthy spiritual liaisons must be repented of and renounced.

In one of Reinhard Bonnke's meetings in Africa, a crippled girl could not be healed until an amulet band that was clasped around her crippled limb was cut off and renounced. Only then could she be healed and set free. That girl was under the power of what the Bible calls witchcraft from an accursed object.

The Blessing versus the Curse

The Bible has a lot to stay about blessings and curses. We can live in either realm—the realm of blessings or of curses. In other words, we can be blessed or we can live under a dark cloud. Deuteronomy 28 is a very important chapter because it describes all the potentialities of both blessings and curses. First-class faith comprehends these spiritual realities and acts accordingly.

The word *curse* may sound like a superstitious old-fashioned word. Think of a curse as disfavor with God, as evil or misfortune that has been invoked or caused. In Deuteronomy 28 sicknesses that result from disobedience are described as curses. The first fourteen verses of the chapter describe all the potential blessings of obedience: if you live according to God's commandments and heed His voice, you and your children will be blessed, coming and going. You will be plenteous in goods; you will be healthy; and you will enjoy more than enough. Yes, you will be disease-free!

Heeding His voice is the key. So, how do you normally hear His voice? God's voice is in His Word. He has spoken and recorded His instructions in the Bible, which is our manufacturer's handbook!

Choose Life

His instructions are for our benefit. Misfortune and evil will befall a person, family, group, region, or nation because of disobedience to God and His precepts. Many live and labor under what the Bible clearly describes as curses, but they do not know it.

After listing all the potential blessings and curses, God said the choice was ours. But He encouraged us to make the right choice for our children and ourselves:

> *This day I call heaven and earth as witnesses against you that I have set before you life and death, blessings and curses. Now choose life, so that you and your children may live* (Deuteronomy 30:19 NIV).

God has graciously given us free will to choose life. He will not force us to live holy lives. He will allow us to do whatever we desire; but if we choose poorly, we will have the devil to pay in the end.

Curses do not happen out of a clear blue sky. Curses have causes. A righteous person might be persecuted for righteousness' sake, but a righteous person is not a curse magnet. In fact, a curse cannot stick to a person who is clean before God. Biblical evidence of this truth is found in Proverbs 26:2: "Like a fluttering sparrow...an undeserved curse does not come to rest" (NIV).

In John 9:2, Jesus' disciples asked Him, "Rabbi, who sinned, this man or his parents, that he was born blind?" (NIV). Although Jesus said that neither sinned, people in Bible days were familiar enough with the Word of God to know what our biblically illiterate generation does not fathom: there are consequences and curses because of sin and disobedience. In their question, the disciples were acknowledging the scriptural truth about the sins of the fathers being visited on the children (see Exod. 34:7).

Yet as a compassionate Healer, Jesus' attitude was summed up later by the apostle Paul in Romans 5:20: "where sin abounded, grace did much more abound...." Jesus looked at the case positively, asserting that the blindness would turn into a miracle, bringing glory to God. Please note that the sickness did not glorify God, but the miraculous healing glorified God.

Doctor Jesus never scratched His head, saying He couldn't do anything. When the Great Physician is on the scene, all things are possible. First-class faith faces these weighty issues and is willing to grapple and come to terms with all the Word of God. We can therefore choose: we can see every sickness and infirmity as something to groan about *or* we can consider it an opportunity to demonstrate the power of God!

If we choose to walk with God, blessings will follow us and our children:

> *I call heaven and earth to witness against you today, that I have set before you life and death, the blessing and the curse. So choose life in order that you may live, you and your descendants* (Deuteronomy 30:19 NASB).

On the other side of the disobedience coin are three basic kinds of curses mentioned in the Scriptures: (1) ancestral (generational) curses, (2) curses caused by personal sins, (3) and regional curses caused by corporate, collective sins. Let's take a closer look at each type.

Ancestral Curses

First we'll look at the generational curses passed down from ancestors. In Exodus 34:7 God warned that the iniquities of one generation would have continued effects, all the way to the third and fourth generations:

Keeping mercy for thousands, forgiving iniquity and transgression and sin, and that will by no means clear the guilty; visiting the iniquity of the fathers upon the children, and upon the children's children, unto the third and to the fourth generation (Exodus 34:7).

After his adultery with Bathsheba, and her resulting pregnancy, David repented with bitter tears in Psalms 51. Nathan the prophet announced the consequences of David's sin in Second Samuel 12:10, saying, "Now therefore, the sword shall never depart from your house..." (NKJV).

Nathan went on to say:

...you shall not die. However, because by this deed you have given great occasion to enemies of the LORD to blaspheme, the child...shall surely die (2 Samuel 12:13-14 NKJV).

The Lord struck the child. Even though David sincerely repented, the decreed judgments were passed down to his children. His household turned to bitter infighting. Some of his sons became treasonous or sick with incest. His own daughter was raped by her brother. David committed sin in secret, but his wives were raped on his rooftop. We must face the harsh reality that although under grace the Lord does forgive (as He also forgave David), nevertheless our actions have consequences, as God has said:

I...am a jealous God, visiting the iniquity of the fathers...to the third and fourth generations of those who hate Me, but showing mercy to thousands, to those who love Me and keep My commandments (Exodus 20:5-6 NKJV).

Clearly, it pays great dividends to serve God faithfully.

Types of Ancestral Curses

Some of the terrible and tragic ancestral curses enunciated in Deuteronomy 28 include:

- Poverty or financial insufficiency
- Barrenness or impotency; miscarriages

- Failure of plans

- Untimely, unnatural deaths

- Sickness and disease, especially chronic, hereditary ailments

- Life traumas, crises

- Mental and emotional breakdowns; divorce

What was the first generational curse? The apostle Paul referenced it in Romans 5:12. He explained that by one man (Adam), sin entered the entire human race and impacted the world. The Fall of Adam and Eve condemned all their descendants; but Christ's Atonement is our remedy. His righteousness freely covers and removes our sins. By faith we can break all generational curses over ourselves, in Messiah's name.

Curses Caused by Personal Sin

There are curses caused by an ancestor's sin, and there are curses of our own making. But even these chains can be broken by Messiah!

Always, we are to worship God and Him only. Therefore, idolatry of any kind brings a curse. The Torah is clear: "Cursed be the man that maketh any graven or molten image, an abomination unto the LORD, the work of the hands of the craftsman, and putteth it in a secret place..." (Deut. 27:15).

Other actions also bring a curse. According to the Law and other teachings of the Lord, the following will put you and your family under a curse:

- Dishonoring parents; striking or cursing parents

- Oppressing the defenseless

- Sexual sins

- Rape

- Conceiving children out of wedlock

- Witchcraft, consulting mediums, fortune-telling, use of horoscopes or Ouija boards (Any occult practice puts you under a curse!)

- Murder and murder-for-hire (includes those paid to perform abortions)

Other biblical passages highlight potential curses: Genesis 12:3 and Numbers 24:9 warn that cursing, lightly esteeming, or mistreating Israel (Abraham's seed) brings a curse and dangerous disfavor with God.

Furthermore, Malachi 2:2 mentions a curse resulting from our failure to give glory to God. Malachi 3:9 and Haggai 1:6-9 reveal that a curse is the consequence of robbing God of tithes and offerings. Malachi 3:7-12 states that the tithe belongs to God; therefore, if you keep it, you are a thief, and you will be "cursed with a cursed" (Mal. 3:9). Many in the Church today are living under this curse. They can be sick and afflicted (along with their children), because they are withholding from God what belongs to Him. Many want to argue stubbornly on this issue. Yet the Lord makes it doubly clear that if you will not tithe, you will be under a curse. Especially note the double use of the word *curse* in this verse: "Ye are *cursed* with a *curse:* for ye have robbed me, even this whole nation" (Mal. 3:9).

Revelation 22:18-19 tells us that taking away or adding to the Word of God will also put you under a curse.

Matthew 18:34-35 teaches that refusing to forgive others legally turns you, your spouse, your children, and your possessions over to the devil.

First-class faith comes to terms with this fact and rectifies it: If you are not living under God's blessings, chances are, you are living under His disfavor (i.e., a curse). Ask the Lord to show you which areas of your life are not pleasing to Him and are therefore accursed.

Curses must be broken because they are associated with a lack of self-control and are often identified by compulsive behavior. Additionally, the

Bible warns us not to bring cursed objects into our home, such as statues, pictures, jewelry, and questionable artifacts (often obtained from foreign countries) that are possibly graven images or objects associated with the occult. Accursed objects defile the atmosphere and attract oppression like magnets, whereas a home free from accursed objects is light and peaceful.

Be careful of the gifts people give you. Do not feel compelled to keep them out of politeness. You might unknowingly accept an accursed object with spirits attached to it.

I personally know several people who were always sick because they collected Buddhas and other Eastern idols in their homes. They had no idea that demonic spirits were attached to the idolatrous decorative objects. One family was given a wooden statue of a beggar. They placed the statue on their porch (out of politeness to a family member who had given the object as a gift). Financial misfortunes befell that house until a discerning minister suggested that the statue be removed and destroyed.

Regional Curses

Regional or national curses are a third category. Proverbs 29:2 declares: "When the righteous are in authority, the people rejoice: but when the wicked beareth rule, the people mourn."

Spain was very powerful until she evicted all of her Jews in 1492. With the Jews expelled, Spain's glory also departed. According to Genesis 12:3, God promises to bless individuals and nations that bless Israel, and declares that those who curse Israel will incur His displeasure.

Spain lost her influence and never enjoyed a revival. But 500 years later in 1992, we were privileged to be part of a national repentance service in Spain. We repented on the nation's behalf for the eviction of its Jews. It is no mere coincidence that Revelation TV, a great voice of end-time truth, is now broadcasting to the world from Spain!

Words That Curse

Curses can be transmitted with our mouths. How we speak about ourselves and our children is so important. A pastor was invited to preach in a prison. He asked one of the young men behind bars, "Why are you here?"

Without hesitating, the prisoner answered, "Because my father said I would never amount to anything, and I have fulfilled his words."

Many curses such as alcoholism have origins in past generations, but the main cause of curses is simply *words*—words that our parents have spoken or that we ourselves have carelessly spoken over our lives and destinies.

Spoken words have power to bless or to curse. The story of the fig tree in Mark 11:14 is the perfect example of how this dynamic works. Jesus told the tree, "No man eat fruit of thee hereafter…." and the disciples heard it. The next day, Peter observed, "Lord, the fig tree You cursed has died" (see Mark 11:20).

It was Jesus' habit to speak life, as He did in John 11:43, saying, "Lazarus, come forth." But Jesus also knew the power of words to bring appropriate judgment, which was His prerogative in the case of the fig tree. Jesus spoke negatively to the tree. Peter recognized that He had cursed it, causing it to die.

How many times have we spoken negatively, not realizing that we were putting word curses on ourselves or others? First-class faith learns to correct our words and to rephrase things. In James 3:6-10 we learn that the tongue is a fire; it defiles the whole body and is set on fire of hell.

But by the power of the Holy Spirit the tongue *can* be controlled. When others speak evil against us, we can say, "I do not receive those curses." Therefore, the Lord will not allow the negative force of those words to influence us, because the curse causeless does not alight (see Prov. 26:2).

In Matthew 5:44 Jesus said, "…Love your enemies, bless them that curse you…pray for them which…persecute you…." He added, "Be ye therefore perfect, even as your Father which is in heaven is perfect" (Matt. 5:48).

Paul echoed Jesus' words when he commanded us to bless others. Paul wrote: "Bless them which persecute you: bless, and curse not" (Rom. 12:14).

These verses show how important our words are. Therefore we must also monitor and correct idle words, as Jesus explained:

> *I say unto you, That every idle word that men shall speak, they shall give account thereof in the day of judgment. For by thy words thou shalt be justified, and by thy words thou shalt be condemned* (Matthew 12:36-37).

Be very diligent to watch what you say. Otherwise, "You are snared with the words of your mouth" (Prov. 6:2 NKJV). The tongue is the most powerful force on earth. We must learn to bridle it.

Telltale Symptoms

Symptoms mentioned or alluded to in Deuteronomy 28 can help to identify any generational or personal curses you may be dealing with. These symptoms include:

- Mental or emotional breakdowns
- Chronic sicknesses, especially hereditary ailments
- Barrenness, tendency to miscarriage, and related female problems
- Breakdown of marriages, family alienations
- Being prone to accidents
- Family history of suicides, other unnatural or untimely deaths in a family
- Confusion and depression
- Financial insufficiency

Poverty is listed under the curses in Deuteronomy 28; prosperity is categorized under the blessings. Many people today do not know whether poverty is a blessing or a virtue; but poverty is clearly described as part of the curse. If God's Word defines poverty as a curse, I will believe His definition rather than the opinion of a theologian who whitewashes poverty.

Children of God are supposed to be living under the blessings, yet so many believers possess zero knowledge about these things! The Bible says we perish for lack of knowledge (see Hos. 4:6). We must learn how to hear from the Holy Spirit. He will tell us if and when we are dealing with curses.

When He reveals the operation of curses in our lives, we need not despair: Jesus became a curse for us so that we might be set free. He endured the curse in darkness and pain on the Cross so that we might enjoy the blessings of Abraham. To be set free, we must repent; we must also renounce the curse by speaking to the mountain (problem) and proclaiming the truth stated in Galatians 3:13: "[Messiah] has redeemed us from the curse of the law, having become a curse for us (for it is written, 'Cursed is everyone who hangs on a tree')…" (NKJV).

Understanding the Blessing of Abraham

Messiah redeemed us in order that the Gentiles might inherit the blessing of Abraham (see Gal. 3:14). But what is the blessing of Abraham? And how can you receive something by faith if you don't know what it is?

The Bible mentions blessings hundreds of times. The blessing of Abraham has come to us through Messiah. Abraham's blessing includes the abundant life, salvation, success, prosperity, long life, and health.

Part of the blessing of Abraham is fellowship with God. Healing flows from fellowship with Him. A Scripture cross-stitched by my grandmother is a family treasure; it quotes Psalms 50:14-15: "Offer unto God thanksgiving; and pay thy vows unto the most High: and call upon me in the day of trouble: I will deliver thee, and thou shalt glorify me."

Surely an aspect of fellowship with God is a thankful heart. How do you feel when you pour yourself out—when you give and give, and nobody thanks you? Yet we often treat God that way. We should continually thank our heavenly Father for His benefits, for such a great salvation that He provided through His Son, Jesus.

Has He healed you? Has He preserved and rescued you? Has He delivered you from trouble? Do not forget to pay your vows and to thank God. It is my belief that if you fail to thank God, He might not repeat the blessing. In First Thessalonians 5:18, the apostle Paul clarified this "attitude of gratitude." He did not instruct us to give thanks *for* everything, but to offer up thanksgiving *in* every situation.

If you are a whiner, grumbler, and complainer; if you never speak to mountains; if you fail to tithe your income; you will just barely scrape by. Life will be miserable! But if you pour out heartfelt gratitude to the Lord; if you command mountains to move; if you pay your tithes and offerings; if you pray for the peace of Jerusalem, you will prosper! (See Psalms 122:6.)

Sadly, in faith battles, most believers tend to give up after a few hours. First-class faith has the presence of mind to rise up with indignation, resist the devil, cast out demons, lay hands on the sick, break curses, remit sins, and speak to the mountain in an authoritative voice.

Don't give up, and the devil will flee. This is first-class faith! Got it?

Points to Ponder

1. To what extent might you be sitting on the fence where healing is concerned? How do your personal beliefs compare with God's will as expressed in His Word?

2. How do the Gospels portray sickness? How should we approach sickness in light of this?

3. Describe any new insights gained into the three kinds of curses discussed. What light does this shed on your own struggles, or the struggles of loved ones?

Notes

1. Biblesoft's New Exhaustive Strong's Numbers and Concordance with Expanded Greek-Hebrew Dictionary, CD-ROM, Biblesoft, Inc. and International Bible Translators, Inc. (1994, 2003, 2006) s.v. "choliy," (OT 2483).

2. Biblesoft's New Exhaustive Strong's Numbers and Concordance with Expanded Greek-Hebrew Dictionary, CD-ROM, Biblesoft, Inc. and International Bible Translators, Inc. (1994, 2003, 2006) s.v. "mak'ob," (OT 4341).

Chapter 3

THE RESTORATION OF HEALING

Acts 3:21 declares that the Lord must remain in heaven until the time of the restoration of all things. The Church has lost much of its original power but these *are* days of restoration!

I've researched the writings of the Christian fathers and other documents of the Church dating from the close of the Apostolic Age up to the seventh century, when the Church was plunged, through doubt and unbelief, into the Dark Ages. But from an examination of these records, it is clear that healing was a part of the Church's ongoing outreach and the healing ministry was inseparable from the proclamation of the kingdom of God!

Today the Lord still expects His followers to heal the sick, raise the dead, and believe Him to do His works and greater works because He sent us the empowerment of the Holy Spirit. The reasons why any church does not heal today must be faced and repented of: they are doubt, unbelief, and a lack of faith. Also, miracles often do not occur simply because they are not expected.

The apostles' own records in the New Covenant continued toward the close of the first century. Healing accompanied preaching and was universally practiced by the apostles and carried on into the second century. Perhaps Origen was the greatest witness for the practice of healing in the third century when evil spirits were expelled, and many cures performed.

In the fourth century, Ambrose and Augustine testified of healings by various means, such as prayer and sacraments, and the relics of martyrs.

I believe it can be argued that there is biblical precedent for the use of relics. In Second Kings 13:21, Elisha's bones were filled with such an anointing that even after he was dead and buried, direct contact with his bones brought a dead man back to life (when the man's corpse was tossed into the prophet's tomb)!

Up to about the fourth century, the Church was not completely apostate. Until the day of Constantine, Church fathers testified to the continuing power of believers to heal. Unfortunately, with the establishment of Christianity as the state religion, heathen practices were mingled in the Church, and apostolic faith was therefore diluted.

However, in every century the Lord has reserved a remnant of believers who have trusted and proven Him as Healer. By the fourth century, the laying on of hands had grown less common. The Church historian Eusebius, Bishop of Caesarea, noted the growing rarity of spiritual gifts, and he attributed the decline to the Church's unworthiness to receive miracles and spiritual gifts.

Ancient liturgies preserve the expectation of supernatural cures. There were many such liturgies, according to evidence outlined in *The Anointing of the Sick in Scripture and Tradition* by F.W. Puller. Puller quotes from the Gregorian Sacramentary (compiled by St. Gregory the Great, Bishop of Rome from AD 590 to 604) regarding the consecration of the oil as "a means of protection for mind and body, for getting rid of all pains, all illnesses, all sickness of the body...."[1]

In the Early Church, our Lord's original command to heal the sick was obeyed and carried out in its literal sense. The ministry of healing was not qualified with the disclaimer "if it be Thy will." The Church had learned from her Master that wholeness, or salvation of both body and soul, is indeed covered by the will of God. This holy conviction found utterance by the frequent double cure description of the Lord in ancient liturgies as "Savior of our souls and bodies," or, "Physician of our souls and bodies."

For example, in the liturgy of Saint Mark, the ministry of healing is honorably upheld: "Master, Lord, and our God, Thou Who didst elect the twelve-lighted lamp of the twelve Apostles, and didst send them into the whole world to preach and to teach the Gospel of Thy kingdom…heal every sickness and every infirmity in the people…."[2]

The Church for several centuries still claimed to be endowed with the charisma of healing, and some faithful ministers continued to exercise power to impart healing. One of the earliest known of these liturgies, *The Testament of Our Lord,* said: "O Christ…Who art the Healer of every sickness and of every suffering…send on this oil…the delivering [power] of Thy good compassion, that it may… heal those who are sick…for Thou art mighty and praised for ever and ever. Amen."

The Irish *Book of Dimma* in the eighth century contained Gospels and an Office for the Communion of the Sick.[3] Prayers for recovery from sickness were unconditional; *the sick person was exhorted to perceive the hand of God in his recovery, rather than in his sickness.* A typical prayer from ancient books was full of faith and devoid of doubt:

> Let us pray, brethren, to Our Lord God for our brother, N, whom present sickness…sorely wounds, that the Lord's kindness may condescend to cure him with heavenly medicine…. O Lord, Holy Father…perform Thy accustomed work….[4]

I especially salute the faith in that clause: "perform Thy *accustomed* work"!

Somebody will always ask, "If healing is God's will, how do you explain the suffering of Job, or Paul's thorn?" These afflictions were surely permitted by God. However, the devil was cited as the author. In Paul's case, he said it was "the messenger of Satan sent to buffet me, lest I should be exalted above measure" (2 Cor. 12:7). And in Job's crucible, Satan was named as the Accuser and culprit. When Job's testing was complete, God restored double blessings to him.

The presumption that we must endure sickness without challenging its trespass on our bodies is a man-made doctrine. We should resist, fight, refuse, and rebuke sickness in Yeshua's name, as He commanded us to do. And if sin is the cause, we should repent and be restored. "If sin is the wound, repentance is the medicine" was the saying of a great saint.

The Glory Departed

Between the seventh and eleventh centuries, the Church forfeited the precious gifts of God and backslid into the Dark Ages. *Ichabod!*

Consider what happened when faith was forfeited and the glory departed: the institutional Church carried on, merely going through the motions of anointing with oil. But because there was little faith (and consequently not many recorded miracles), the biblical instruction in James 5 to anoint the sick with oil devolved into the sacrament of Extreme Unction, as part of the Last Rites. This anointing became a ritual, not for healing and raising up an individual, but for consolation of the dying! How ironic!

When Martin Luther and the Reformation arrived on the scene in Western Christianity, the Christian world had largely lost consciousness of healing as part of the Atonement, but also—dangerously—salvation was no longer understood as the free gift of God obtained by faith in Jesus.

The Church had substituted the true Gospel with doctrines of works and indulgences. The glory of the Cross was covered by a spiritual fog. Thank God that the Protestant Church under Luther and other brave reformers recovered much of Gospel truth. But the healing arm of salvation was not yet restored.

How far the Church had drifted from the power of apostolic times! "The just shall live by faith" was a great recovery of truth concerning salvation. But the just shall *also* live by faith concerning healing!

The reformers Martin Luther, John Knox, and John Calvin recorded isolated cases of healings. Some advances toward recovery were made later in the ministry of the great British apostle and evangelist John Wesley. In his journals, Wesley recorded 240 cases of healings of every class of disease. Wesley also recorded instances of casting out devils, and people falling down under the power of the Holy Spirit. However, these incidents were not perceived as God's norm, but as exceptional cases.

We are still on the road to the recovery of *all things,* including Yah's calendar, although great strides were made in the last century to restore the healing aspects of the Gospel. It's been said that the greatest of spiritual men are but infants prattling around on the shores of the great sea of eternal light, life and power, compared to what the early church actually possessed and revealed.

His Glory Restored

The Early Church saw great miracles, but even what the Early Church achieved does not set our boundaries! All things continue to be possible to those who believe and to those led by the Holy Spirit! We are not limited to experiences recorded in the Acts of the Apostles!

Miracles continue today, and many have been documented in my book, *Miracles Among Muslims: The Jesus Visions*. Extraordinary miracles are taking place in the Islamic world as a testimony to the Holy Spirit drawing into the kingdom of God precious Muslim Background Believers! By the grace and calling of God, outstanding healings are also happening in our own ministry in the Muslim world and beyond through the prayer of agreement, the laying on of hands, the anointing with oil, and supernatural phenomena involving dreams. For example, Muslim Background Believers with whom I have prayed have been visited by the Lord and healed in dreams.

The modern recovery of healing can be traced to pioneers such as Dr. A.B. Simpson, founder of the Missionary Alliance; the Reverend Andrew Murray of South Africa who was healed of an incurable "preacher's throat"; Dr. John Alexander Dowie, who in 1901 established a city in the USA for people who trusted Jesus only as their Physician. John G. Lake was greatly anointed in his ministry to Africa so that dreaded diseases seemed to bounce off his body during epidemics. He demonstrated that fear absorbs germs, but faith repels them. Smith Wigglesworth, called the "Apostle of Faith," was a spiritual giant in the last century in England who recovered much of apostolic faith concerning healing. Other healing pioneers included Rees Howells of Wales; the Americans, A.A. Allen and Oral Roberts who, after being healed of tuberculosis, especially pioneered in the recovery of laying on of hands.

Because a sign of the Last Days is the outpouring of the Holy Spirit on handmaidens and women, it is not surprising that a number of brave and bold women helped to restore the truth about healing. One was a European, Dorothea Trudel, whose healing institution was licensed and considered apostolic in her day. Another, Dorothy Kerin, founded the Christ the Healer Church in Burrswood, Kent, in the United Kingdom after being cured of tubercular meningitis (a fatal condition in her day). I believe that the most influential woman in divine healing in the United States in the 1800s was Carrie Judd Montgomery, whose book *The Prayer of Faith*, is one of the best I've ever read on the subject of divine healing. She was raised up off of a deathbed because of James 5: 14-15. Mrs. Montgomery helped recover the doctrine of healing in the Atonement and initiated healing homes. She believed that once the prayer of faith is done, healing is assured even if symptoms linger.

Other female healing pioneers include Aimee Semple McPherson and Kathryn Kuhlman, who was a forerunner in the recovery of healing by the word of knowledge. Kuhlman visited many of the tents of healing evangelists in the 1940s. In at least two books about her life it is documented that she was greatly distressed at the way evangelists put the blame on the people for their lack of faith when they were not healed. Miss Kuhlman bemoaned this as an injustice and cried, "They have taken away my Lord, and I know not where they have laid him."[5] Kuhlman also greatly contended against unbelief in her day. She said, "I knew that if I lived and died and never saw a single healing miracle like the apostles experienced in the Book of Acts, it would not change God's Word."[6] Later, after her healing ministry was established, she was always distressed that, despite her high success rate, not all were healed. She campaigned for believers to keep the standard high, where Jesus placed it.

We must keep persevering to recover and maintain the healing message!

End-time Anointing

Pioneers in the recovery of the truth concerning healing had in common the gift of faith and a willingness to yield to the Holy Spirit. Obeying the Lord is more important than people's many objections to divine healing. All of these pioneers were forerunners of the healing recovery we are enjoying today; and because of their breaker anointing, they are worthy of double honor, despite often being the targets of ridicule.

One of the signs of the Lord's soon appearing is the outpouring of the Holy Spirit on all flesh and the restoration of the gifts of the Spirit, including the gift of faith, the gift of working miracles, and the gifts of healing. A time of restoration even greater than the Early Church is expected by many healing evangelists, although I am deeply challenged by our Lord's own prophetic question about whether, when the Son of Man comes, He will find faith on the earth (see Luke 18:8). Just as the occult increases to counterfeit the gifts of the Spirit, so the anointing of the Holy Spirit *should* be greater upon the Bride of Christ, who is being prepared without spot or blemish—a whole, "sickless" testimony to the greater works of Jesus. You do not want to miss being part of the end-time restoration of God's healing!

Ask, Seek, Knock

Doubt and unbelief are more dangerous now because of the large accumulation of miracle testimonies in our time. If we will be realistic, we can conclude that many of our problems stem from a lack of faith. Jesus said, "If you can believe, all things are possible to him who believes" (Mark 9:23 NKJV).

There is a lazy misconception among many believers today: "If God wants me to have it, He'll just give it to me."

No! God instructs us to *ask, seek, and knock* (see Matt. 7:7). God has already given us everything in His Word, which contains exceeding great and precious promises. I believe we must wrestle these promises away from the devil as we fight the fight of faith. Relentlessly, Satan tries to steal God's Word from believers. Demonic forces challenge us with sickness, disease, and problems; so we must go on the offensive to take the kingdom by violently (rigorously) resisting (see Matt. 11:12).

Holy Violence

We must exert effort to be real believers. We must rise up in indignation against the forces of darkness. In Matthew 11:12 Jesus declared: "And from the days of John the Baptist until now the kingdom of heaven suffereth violence, and the violent take it by force."

What a verse! The Lord meant that the Gospel would suffer violence from the persecutions of its enemies who oppose and contradict it, reproaching and intimidating disciples, and seeking to take away the very life of Messiah. But on the other hand, there would be those who would forcefully take the kingdom.

In this verse commentators say the Lord referred to publicans, harlots, and Gentile sinners—people despised as intruders who nevertheless were voraciously in love with Christ, eagerly desirous of His salvation and of communion with Him. They grabbed greedily (not in a negative sense) the salvation and healing that were freely offered by Jesus. Many embraced Him wholeheartedly while being willing to submit to the most violent deaths to obtain the resurrection.

We used to know a Jewish boxer who became a follower of Jesus. Burt Singer, of blessed memory, was his name. He became a full-time preacher along with his wife, Pam. Often when I would see Burt, I would exhort him to expound upon Matthew 11:12 ("the kingdom of heaven suffereth violence"). With great delight, Burt would go into preacher mode, making his hands into fists and expounding with marvelous, energetic exhortations about how we must become offensive and fight off the devil and all opposition.

In the days of Jesus, the common people had an intense desire to draw close to the Savior to the point that they pressed upon Him. No doubt, some of the weaker ones were pushed down and even trodden upon in the rush to be near Jesus and to receive His touch. As our Savior witnessed all the jostling, He said, in effect, "As you press and throng around Me, elbowing one another, even so must it be if you would be saved, for the gate that leads to life is narrow, and few there be that find it" (see Matt. 7:13-14).

Imagine a crowd of souls so anxious to reach Yeshua. He Himself warned that unless they exhibited such earnestness, they would never come into real saving contact with Him; but if, on the other hand, they were truly sincere in finding Him and having close encounters with Him, they would certainly be saved.

"But," you might ask, "isn't salvation all about the grace of God?" Yes, indeed it is, but when God's Spirit begins to strive with us and to draw us into the kingdom, we also begin to strive to obtain all the promises of God. That is why we forcefully speak to mountains to be moved!

There is a spiritual *jihad* (the Arabic word for "struggle")—not a physical *jihad* of terrorism and killing, but a spiritual *jihad* of all true believers, meaning that we struggle daily against the evil inclination. We don't wrestle against human beings but we struggle and wrestle against powers of darkness in heavenly places.

Wrestling is a down-and-dirty, close-contact activity. Yet in the West there is so much preaching about ease and success. Somebody has said that if Jesus had preached what Western preachers preach today, He never would have been crucified!

In Acts 14:22, Paul and Barnabas exhorted disciples to continue in the faith, saying "we must through much tribulation enter into the kingdom of God." Moreover, Psalms 34:19 states a fact of life: "Many are the afflictions of the righteous, but the Lord delivereth him out of them all."

The Good News is that when we are yoked to the Lord, there is an ease in the Spirit walk. His yoke is easy and his burden is light (see Matt. 11:30) because His presence grants supernatural assistance, wisdom, and strength.

Give Thanks

Furthermore, God responds to thankful hearts. Gratitude is not just an attitude for Thanksgiving Day; thanksgiving should become a daily habit in every believer's life. *Most days I take time to thank the Lord for another day of health!* I am so grateful for every day that is free from sickness and disease. Because we live in a fallen world, I am deeply grateful for the Lord's faithful protection and preservation.

I learned an important declaration as I frequently watched the evangelist, Reinhard Bonnke, pray for afflicted persons. As I assisted in the healing lines, I heard him say, "Lord, thank You for Your healing anointing surging through this body, driving out all affliction from head to toe!"

That is a great general declaration for all of us to make over our bodies from time to time. I have never forgotten that powerful confession about driving out affliction to keep the anointing moving in our bodies. Reinhard always prays for the sick after preaching his salvation messages because he firmly believes that healing is part and parcel of the Atonement. I also include prayer for physical needs in our Gospel meetings because the full Gospel must be preached.

What about Physicians?

As we restore the healing arm of the Gospel, we must have a clear understanding about the medical profession and its limitations. What does the Bible say about physicians? On the whole, Scripture considers healing as a divine monopoly. One of God's covenant names is The LORD Your Physician (see Exod. 15:26). Yeshua was the ultimate Healer, the Physician par excellence. Jesus indirectly called Himself a doctor when He stated in Mark 2:17 that it "is not the healthy who need a doctor, but the sick. I have not come to call the righteous, but sinners" (NIV).

King Asa in the Old Testament became diseased in his feet and died because he sought the physicians and not the Lord (see 2 Chron. 16:12). The woman with the issue of blood in the New Testament spent all of her money on doctors but only grew worse, until she touched the fringe of Jesus' garment (see Luke 8:43-44).

Luke was described as the "beloved physician" in Colossians 4:14 and was a close travel companion of Saint Paul. But nowhere in the Scriptures do we read that Paul consulted Dr. Luke on behalf of the sick. No text suggests that Paul asked, "Dr. Luke, please give a diagnosis and medicate these people." No, rather, we see Paul commanding and healing people in Jesus' name. Dr. Luke was the scribe who faithfully recorded the exploits of the apostles.

Undoubtedly doctors and nurses are often part of God's healing provision. The best in the medical profession do many noble deeds. Physicians receive a "thumbs up" in the apocryphal book, Ecclesiasticus (Wisdom of Sirach), a book accepted as part of the biblical canon in Roman Catholic, Anglican, Coptic, Eastern Orthodox, and most Oriental Orthodox churches. "Honour the physician for the need thou hast of him: for the most High hath created him. For all healing is from God, and he shall receive gifts of the king. The skill of the physician shall lift up his head, and in the sight of great men he shall be praised. The most High hath created medicines out of the earth, and a wise man will not abhor them. Was not bitter water made sweet with wood?" (Sirach 38:1-5)

Sirach was a Jewish scribe who lived in Jerusalem in the second century before Christ. The Wisdom of Sirach was also included in the Septuagint (the Hebrew Bible translated into Greek). The Wisdom of Sirach influenced early Christianity as it was explicitly cited in the Epistle of James, the Didache, and the Epistle of Barnabas. Clement of Alexandria and Origen quoted from it repeatedly. The book is sometimes called Ecclesiasticus because it was read frequently in the churches.

However, in Sirach 38:15, the theological link between sickness and sin is maintained: "He that sinneth in the sight of his Maker, shall fall into the hands of the physician." Sirach allowed calling for a physician, yet he also preserved the divine character of healing. He advised in chapter 38, verses 9 through 11, that every devout person when sick should pray to God, repent from sin, resolve to amend his ways, and offer gifts and sacrifices in the Temple. Sirach also specified that the doctor should begin with a prayer to diagnose the sickness correctly, to alleviate the pain, and to save the patient's life.

In Old Testament Scripture, the Levites functioned not only as ministers of the sanctuary but also in the role of physicians. They were given strict quarantine laws by God. Circumcisions were commanded to be held on the eighth day after birth, the ideal day because of the development of Vitamin K and also the peaking of a blood-clotting protein in the blood.

The Levites were given the duties of ministering in the Tabernacle, and later in the Temple, performing the services necessary to keep Israel free from sin and contaminating sickness. All atonement for Israel was made so that God could dwell in their midst. The priests not only made atonement for the nation but also for the sins of individuals so that no plague would break out among the people. Always in the Scriptures, sickness and plagues were connected with sin and rebellion. God had covenanted to take away sickness, if the people were obedient. He promised to keep His obedient children in perfect health. (See Exodus 15:26; Deuteronomy 28.) Psalms 105:37 attests that there was not a feeble person in all of the tribes. Therefore healing and health were provided by the Mosaic Covenant, and continued in the lives of the prophets.

Elijah and Elisha, for example, both raised the dead. *In the fullness of time when Jesus appeared, He confirmed and carried on the same program of divine health.* Yeshua instructed cured lepers to report to the priests for medical examination according to the Law of Moses. The apostles carried on the ministry of healing with many signs and wonders.

The Name, the Blood

When we pray for healing, we should pray in the name of Jesus. In Hebrew thought, the name of a person is synonymous with the person's character. Jesus/Yeshua means "God is salvation" (i.e., saving health). When we pray in His name, we are praying in the name of saving health. "God be merciful unto us, and bless us; and cause his face to shine upon us; Selah. That thy way may be known upon earth, thy saving health [salvation] among all nations" (Ps. 67:1-2). "Your salvation" or "your saving health," is literally "your Jesus/Yeshua" (ye·shu·'a·te·cha). His name signifies a Savior of Yehovah's appointing and sending. Yeshua came to obtain salvation and health for all nations as the Physician of souls. His blood is the balm that cures every sin and disease. Although not hidden, this fact was unknown in the nations until the Gospel was proclaimed.

The Bible does not have a lot to say about other human physicians. Two previously mentioned references were negative: In the Tanach (the Jewish Bible), King Asa died because he consulted the physicians rather than God. In the New Testament, the woman with the issue of blood had spent all of her money on physicians, but she only grew worse. She herself was drained, but she drew healing virtue from physical contact with the Lord.

Hungarian Oxfordian scholar Geza Vermes made the following insightful statement in his book *Jesus the Jew*:

> On the whole, Scripture considers healing as a divine monopoly. Recourse to the services of a doctor in preference to prayer is held to be evidence of lack of faith, an act of irreligiousness meriting punishment. This attitude is reflected as late as the third century b.c....in connection with the grave illness of Asa, king of Judah....In general, it can be asserted that to refer certain matters of health to a priest was a duty; to seek the help of a prophet was an act of religion; and to visit the doctor was an act of impiety.[7]

What a statement! "To visit the doctor was an act of impiety!" Most doctor-reliant people in the Church today would pour scorn on this Bible-based statement. And yet the tenor of Scripture is undoubtedly that trusting in the arm of flesh rather than trusting the Lord *is* indeed an act of impiety!

After news of a plane crash, many typically vow, "I'll never fly again!" But why not the same dread of hospitals? An article by Dr. Barbara Starfield of the Johns Hopkins School of Hygiene and Public Health stated that medical errors are the third leading cause of death in the United States. According to the article, there are 12,000 deaths every year from unnecessary surgery; 7,000 deaths per year from medication errors in hospitals; 20,000 deaths every year from other hospital errors; 80,000 deaths annually from hospital infections; 106,000 deaths annually from adverse effects of medications. These figures total up to 225,000 deaths annually in the United States from iatrogenic causes (a term used when a patient dies as a direct result of treatment).[8]

Furthermore, a study revealed that pharmaceutical drugs killed more people than traffic accidents.[9] Just as cigarettes carry a health warning, so a warning that hospitals could be hazardous to your health should be plastered over their doors!

We thank God for the genuine help of hospitals, but we also must seriously rethink unnecessary procedures and rely more on the healing power and promises of the Lord. We have a Great Physician who wants to be trusted and *believed!*

Members of His Body

The founder of the Christian and Missionary Alliance, A.B. Simpson, wrote the classic book, *The Gospel of Healing.* Simpson testified:

> I know not how to account for this [strength] unless it be the imparted life of the dear Lord Jesus in my body....I believe He is pleased in His great condescension to unite Himself with our bodies, and I am persuaded that His body, which is perfectly human and real, can somehow share its vital elements with our organic life, and quicken us from His Living Heart and indwelling Spirit. I find that "...the body is for the Lord, and the Lord for the body...."[10]

Indeed, "we are members of [Christ's] body, of his flesh, and of his bones" (Eph. 5:30). This is a mystery, truly a revelation, which when comprehended, has immense strength and endless power. A foreshadowing of this supernatural power was the strange strength of Bible strongman, Samson. His supernatural strength was not his own but was imparted by the Spirit of the Lord (see Judg. 14:6).

Here is another great divine health key to grasp when recovering the healing message of the Gospel: With the regular measure of faith, we petition the Father for healing. *But when we possess the gift of faith, there is often no petitioning to the Father for healing. Rather, there is a unity with the Godhead and a knowing during which we, like Jesus and the apostles, simply command healing and it is done.*

If you study closely the apostles' activity in the Book of Acts, you don't see them praying for people to be healed. Rather, you see them commanding healing and miracles because they had already fasted and prayed as a lifestyle. That being said, wisdom is continually needed in recovering the healing ministry. I used to lay hands on anything that moved! But overzealousness can be out of order, even destructive. We do not want to bring a reproach upon the ministry of divine healing. We can be guilty of laying hands suddenly on someone who is not ready or even willing to be healed.

There is an order to the New Testament ordinance of healing; it is outlined in James 5:14: "Is any sick among you? let him call for the elders of the church...." *Therefore generally speaking it is the sick person's responsibility to request prayer.* Many times anxious family and friends want me to pray for somebody who has not requested prayer and who does not have the faintest desire for prayer. Praying for them can be presumptuous.

Forgiveness and Healing, Together

The Lord is a willing Healer. The Old Testament prescribes two or three witnesses for a matter to become established, but the case of healing in the New Covenant has more than 100 witnesses!

The word translated "saved" in the New Testament is *sozo.* It is found 120 times in 103 verses and is translated five main ways: *saved, healed, made whole, delivered* and *preserved.*[11] Keep these manifold meanings in mind when you meditate on Romans 10:9: "If you confess with your mouth, 'Jesus is Lord,' and believe in your heart that God raised Him from the dead, you will be saved" [cured, get well, made well, made whole, preserved, recovered, restored, delivered from penalties of judgment, rescued from danger or destruction!] (NIV).

In John 20:23, the Great Commission's emphasis is to remit, or to cancel the sin debt of a person. But we have also been empowered to heal and to raise the dead! Therefore we have been given power and authority from Jesus to say both "Your sins are canceled," and "Arise, take up your bed and walk!"

Which of these authoritative statements is easier to say—"Your sins are forgiven," or "Be healed"? The truth is that both require simple faith to declare. We receive the Lord our Savior by faith, but we also receive the Lord our Healer by faith. We must believe on the Lord Jesus and repent to be saved. We also must repent and believe Him to be healed.

Walking Confidently

Concerning healing, Abba Father made a covenant and gave His will in His covenant name, *Yehovah Physician*, in Exodus 15:26. It is therefore ignorance of God's Word to believe anything else. But there are conditions to walking in divine health. Exodus 15:26 declares: "If you will give earnest heed to the voice of the LORD your God, and do what is right in His sight, and give ear to His commandments, and keep all His statues, I will put none of the diseases on you which I have put on the Egyptians, for I, the LORD, am [Yehovah Rapha] your healer [Physician]" (NASB).

Therefore, to walk in faith, I believe we must have no outstanding issues with God. "Beloved if our heart condemn us not, then have we confidence toward God" (1 John 3:21). To walk in faith, we must also be confident. Confidence is free and fearless, cheerful, bold, marked by assurance and deportment without ambiguity. "And this is the confidence that we have in him, that, if we ask any thing according to his will, he heareth us: and if we know that he hear us, whatsoever we ask, we know that we have the petitions that we desired of him" (1 John 5:14-15).

Are Healed and *Were* Healed

"By his stripes we *are* healed" (Isa. 53:5 NKJV). The prophet penned these words before Christ's work was accomplished. After the Cross, the verse was quoted in the past tense by Peter: "...by whose stripes [we] *were* healed" (1 Pet. 2:24 NKJV).

If we *were* healed, then we *are* healed!

And here is another important Gos-pill: "He sent his word, and healed them, and delivered them from their destructions" (Ps. 107:20). "The word" referred to may be a message sent by a human messenger, such as Isaiah's message to King Hezekiah in his sickness (see 2 Kings 20:4-5; Isa. 38:4). It could be a thought suggested to the mind either directly by God the Holy Spirit, or by an angel, such as in Job 33:23-24. Most often it is a verse from the actual Word of God that comes to us from our memory banks because we have stored up the *rhema* (living) words of Scripture.

For example, some of my favorite fall-back verses for healing are part of the "benefit package" found in Psalms 103:2-5:

> *Bless the LORD, O my soul, and forget not all His benefits: who for-gives all your iniquities* [notice the order: forgiveness first, then healing follows], *who heals all your diseases, who redeems your life from destruction, who crowns you with lovingkindness and tender mer-cies, who satisfies your mouth with good things, so that your youth is re-newed like the eagle's* (NKJV).

Holy Communion

Holy Communion is the "children's bread" and is a big key to the restoration of healing. The Lord's Table is the meal that heals. Although God has provided a number of methods of healing, such as the laying on of hands, surely one of the most precious opportunities for healing can be found at the Lord's Table.

Holy Communion is a powerful source of healing that is unfortu-nately not mentioned in many denominations as a potential cure. I re-ceived Holy Communion growing up in the Presbyterian Church, but never was taught that the meal was related to health.

Primarily, Communion proclaims the Lord's death until He comes, but as I began to study the ministry of healing, I discovered the provi-sion of healing that His death proclaims!

According to First Corinthians 11:28-30, sickness and even prema-ture death can result from not recognizing or discerning the body of the Lord when receiving the Lord's Table. Therefore the manner in which a believer receives the elements of Holy Communion can either ameliorate *or* adversely affect health. We must discern that the cup rep-resents His blood, which was shed for our sins. The bread is emblematic of His body broken for our sicknesses and diseases.

Some believers receive Holy Communion frequently. Some claim to receive it daily. There are also believers who take Communion at home. There are no biblical restrictions on when and where to receive Com-munion. First Corinthians 11:26 states: "For *as often* as ye eat this bread, and drink this cup, ye do shew the Lord's death till he come."

When remembering and proclaiming His death and sacrifice, it is only natural to receive by faith (along with the meal) His healing virtue that He purchased for us at Calvary. "Then Jesus said unto them, Verily, verily, I say unto you, Except ye eat the flesh of the Son of man, and drink his blood, ye have no life in you. Whoso eateth my flesh and drinketh my blood hath eternal life; and I will raise him up at the last day. For my flesh is meat indeed, and my blood is drink indeed" (John 6:53-55).

The converse of the message conveyed in this passage would be this: if we eat His flesh and drink His blood, we *do* have His life within us!

He Took Our Sins and Sicknesses

One of the greatest statements concerning the restoration of the healing aspect of the Gospel was made by Greek scholar Dr. T.J. Mc-Crossan in his book *Bodily Healing and the Atonement*:

> Every saint has a blood-bought right to be healed, but thousands do not know that they must exercise the very same appropriating faith in the bruised body of Christ for their healing as they formerly exercised in His shed blood for their salvation.[12]

Important healing verses to soak in are Matthew 8:16-17:

> *When evening came, they brought to Him many who were demon-possessed; and He cast out the spirits with a word, and healed **all** who were ill. This was to fulfill what was spoken through Isaiah the prophet: "HE HIMSELF TOOK OUR INFIRMITIES AND CARRIED AWAY OUR DISEASES"* (NASB).

Yeshua absorbed, as it were, our sins and sicknesses, during and even before the ordeal of the Cross. This transference of our sins and sicknesses was mysteriously absorbed into His body. Virtue went out of Him, and He wrought miracles at His own expense. The thought is far-reaching, and implies that He bore the ultimate cause of sickness, the sin of the world (see John 1:29). Also, each miracle of healing meant a fresh realization of what bearing the sin of the world would mean. Selah. At the

Cross, He took our sins and gave us freedom; He took our sicknesses and gave us health; He took our poverty and gave us abundance.

Furthermore, ancient rabbis believed the Suffering Servant prophecy of Isaiah 53 rightly described Messiah. In one of their ancient commentaries, Messiah was described as a leper.[13] In an ancient rabbinic commentary, God is represented asking Messiah, "wilt thou bear chastisements"[14] in order to remove the iniquities of the children of God (as written in Isaiah: "surely he hath borne our griefs"). And He replied, "I will bear them with *joy.*"[15] Although this rabbinic commentary is extra-biblical, it nevertheless accurately describes the spirit of the Servant Messiah, Yeshua Himself, as Hebrews 12:2 also describes: "…Jesus, the founder and perfecter of our faith, who for the *joy* that was set before him endured the cross, despising the shame, and is seated at the right hand of the throne of God" (ESV).

Persevere in Healing

The healing message needs regular review. If we do not stay on top of it, we become vulnerable to the eroding power of doubt and unbelief. Like everything else, we must keep eating the Lord's Word concerning healing to remain strong in this area and to be one of the faithful believers who fully recovers the great truth about God's will to heal.

Today, I invite you to take the vitamin of Hebrews 11:6: "Without faith it is impossible to please Him, for he who comes to God must believe that He is, and that He is a rewarder of those who diligently seek Him" (NKJV).

Consider also the power of resisting sickness. James 4:7 declares: "Submit yourselves…to God. Resist the devil, and he will flee from you." The devil is a stubborn foe. Healing is ours, but we have to fight the fight of faith. We must command the devil to vacate. Some believers will not persevere; they will stop trusting God's promises when the devil puts up a fight. But when we become fully convinced of God's promises, the devil is defeated. In the Greek text of this verse, the word *submit* is "a military term meaning 'to arrange [troop divisions] in a military fashion under the command of a leader'"[16], to arrange oneself in subjection. To *resist* essentially means to set oneself against, or withstand, or oppose.[17] To *flee* means to take flight, to avoid as something abhorrent, such as the blood of Jesus being abhorrent to the devil.

We must not back down when the enemy rises up. He is our defeated foe!

The Finished Work

When Jesus cried from the Cross, "It is finished!" He meant that the work of our healing *and* our salvation from sin was completed! "When he had received the [vinegar, Yeshua] said, 'It is finished.' With that, he bowed his head and gave up his spirit" (John 19:30 NIV).

In the New Testament, "It is finished" is a Greek clause also meaning, "The sin debt is paid in full." Hallelu-Yah to the Lamb! "It is finished" meant, "My suffering: the purchase of man's redemption is done." "It is finished!" was surely the Victor's cry. Again I ask: What was finished? The Law was fulfilled as the Lord was obedient unto death, even the death of the Cross. Old Testament prophecies were fulfilled and our redemption was completed. He has "finished the transgression, and made an end of sins, and reconciliation for iniquity, and brought in everlasting righteousness, sealed up the vision and prophecy, and anointed the most Holy" (see Dan. 9:24). His life was not taken from Him by force, but it was freely offered. As the list below explains, there are five categories of wounds that Jesus experienced on our behalf in the Atonement. Because of His holy work on the Cross, there is no physical or mental wound that cannot be healed.

1. *Bruises* are damaged tissues and blood vessels under the skin. (The bruises from the Lord's smiting and scourging provide the antidote for your bruises.)

2. *Scrapes* are painful areas where the outer layer of skin is rubbed off, exposing nerve endings. (Yeshua's scrapes from

carrying the crossbeam and falling in the street, provide substitutionary healing for all of your scrapes and infections.)

3. *Avulsions* occur when a piece of skin is torn away. Yeshua suffered more than thirty-nine stripes. (If it was indeed His burial shroud, there are 120 wounds by two Roman scourges on the Shroud of Turin.) By His avulsions you are also healed of any and all diseases.

4. *Punctures* are caused by a pointed object piercing the skin. I believe the thorns and nails pierced Jesus so that we will mourn for our sins, look to Him, and be saved and healed. Sufferings from the cap of thorns provide a substitution for any sickness having to do with the mind or head, externally or internally. I often say the Lord bore the crown of thorns in the Atonement as a substitution for our mental torments such as depression and downheartedness.

5. *Cuts* are caused by blows or sharp objects that open the skin. They can have either jagged or smooth edges. (The Roman spear opened Yeshua's side from which flowed the redemptive fluids of blood and water.) Whatever you are suffering, by the all-encompassing wounds of Jesus, you *were* healed (see Isa. 53:5; 1 Pet. 2:24). Be healed of your infirmities in Jesus' name.

Points to Ponder

1. When you look to God for your healing, do you add any disclaimers, such as, "If it be Your will"? Biblically speaking, is the disclaimer in line with truth? Why or why not?

2. What qualities did the twentieth-century "pioneers" possess that caused them to be used in the recovery of healing truths? How is this instructive to you?

3. Explain the meaning of Christ's finished work in your life? How does it relate to forgiveness of sin and to healing?

Notes

1. F.W. Puller, *The Anointing of the Sick in Scripture and Tradition* (London: Society for Promoting Christian Knowledge, 1904), 125.
   http://books.google.com/books?id=CF4NAAAAYAAJ& pg=PA125&dq=A+means+of+protection+for+mind+an d+body,+for+getting+rid&hl=en&sa=X&ei=Cxd- wUoaPH9KfkQf6xoEY&ved=0CEgQ6AEwAQ#v=on epage&q=A%20means%20of%20protection%20for%20m ind%20and%20body%2C%20for%20getting%20rid&f=fal se (accessed October 29, 2013).

2. Rev. J.M. Neale, M.A., *The Liturgies of S. Mark, S. James, S. Clement, S. Chrysostom, and the Church of Malabar* (London: J.T. Hayes, Lyall Place, Eaton Square, 1859), 4.
   http://books.google.com/books?id=q5UKAQAA- MAAJ&pg=PA4&dq=Master,+Lord+and+our+God,+ Thou+Who+didst+elect+the+twelve-lighted+ lamp+of+the+twelve&hl=en&sa=X&ei=uxdwUof7N MqlkQfHz4HYDg&ved=0CDkQ6AEwAg#v=onepage &q=Master%2C%20Lord%20and%20our%20God%2C% 20Thou%20Who%20didst%20elect%20the%20twelve- lighted%20lamp%20of%20the%20twelve&f=false (ac- cessed October 29, 2013).

3. "Book of Dimma," *Wikipedia.com,*
   http://en.wikipedia.org/wiki/Book_of_dimma (accessed December 19, 2013).

4. James Moore Hickson, *Heal the Sick,* (New York: E.P. Dut- ton and Co., 1924), xx.

5. Kathryn Kuhlman, Jamie Buckingham, *Daughter of Destiny: The Only Authorized Biography…Kathryn Kuhlman* (Alachua, FL: Bridge-Logos, 1999), 108.
   http://books.google.com/books?id=_0bLppKEMK0C&pg =PA108&dq=They+have+taken+away+my+Lord,+and+I +know+not+where+they+have+laid+him+kathryn+kuhl man&hl=en&sa=X&ei=qiNwUoPhGsmGkQf794CgAQ

&ved=0CC8Q6AEwAA#v=onepage&q=They%20have%
20taken%20away%20my%20Lord%2C%20and%20I%20kn
ow%20not%20where%20they%20have%20laid%20him%20
kathryn%20kuhlman&f=false (accessed October 29, 2013).

6. Ibid., 109.

7. Géza Vermès, *Jesus the Jew: A Historian's Reading of the Gospels* (First Fortress Press, 1981), 59-60.

8. Barbara Starfield, "Is US Health Really the Best in the World?" http://silver.neep.wisc.edu/~lakes/iatrogenic.pdf (accessed December 19, 2013).

9. Reid Wilson, "Drug overdoses kill more people than auto accidents in 29 states," *The Washington Post, Gov Beat,* http://www.washingtonpost.com/blogs/govbeat/wp/20
13/10/08/drug-overdoses-kill-more-people-than-auto-accidents-in-29-states/ (accessed December 19, 2013).

10. Rev. A.B. Simpson, *The Gospel of Healing* (New York: Christian Alliance Publishing Co., 1890), 57, PDF. http://www.cmalliance.org/resources/archives/down-loads/simpson/the-gospel-of-healing.pdf (accessed October 30, 2013).

11. Biblesoft's New Exhaustive Strong's Numbers and Concordance with Expanded Greek-Hebrew Dictionary, CD-ROM, Biblesoft, Inc. and International Bible Translators, Inc. (1994, 2003, 2006) s.v. "sozo," (NT 4982).

12. Dr. T.J. McCrossan, *Bodily Healing and the Atonement* (Broken Arrow, OK: Kenneth Hagin Ministries, 1982).

13. Babylonian Talmud, Sanhedrin 98b.

14. Ibid.

15. Ibid.

16. *Thayer and Smith "Greek lexicom entry for Hupotasso," Bible StudyTools.com;* http://www.biblestudytools.com/lexicons/greek/kjv/hupotasso.html (accessed December 19, 2013).

17. Biblesoft's New Exhaustive Strong's Numbers and Concordance with Expanded Greek-Hebrew Dictionary, CD-ROM, Biblesoft, Inc. and International Bible Translators, Inc. (1994, 2003, 2006) s.v. "anthistemi," (NT 436).

Chapter 4

Hindrances to Healing

Now concerning faith for healing, faith can be resident in the minister, or manifested in the sick person who needs the healing. Sometimes, neither the minister nor the sick person possesses any outstanding faith, yet God manifests His goodness in healing the person!

I have seen people in Gospel meetings in Africa and Asia (particularly Muslims) healed by the power of God through confirming signs and wonders, when they were not exhibiting any apparent faith. They were just part of the crowd needing to learn about Jesus. They were taught that He had healed them, and they were urged to receive Him as their Lord and Savior.

In most cases we know from the Word that without faith nobody is able to please God or to receive anything from Him (see Heb. 11:6; James 1:7). When Jesus rebuked His disciples during a storm on the Sea of Galilee, He said, with great exasperation, "Where is your faith?"

Many times I have also felt the Holy Spirit rise up with indignation, as I have wanted to blurt in the presence of unbelief: "Where is your faith? Can't you find a scripture for your situation?"

Why Does God Allow Sickness?

Having faith is key, but understanding the reasons for sickness is also important. Why does God allow us to become sick in the first place? Let's explore some common reasons:

1. When they are healed, sicknesses and diseases bring glory to the Lord. In John 9:1-7, Jesus healed a man who was blind from birth. Jesus explained that neither the man nor his parents had sinned, but the man was born blind so that the workings of Yehovah should be made manifested (displayed, demonstrated) in him. The Lord did not mean that the man and his parents were sin-free but that a particular sin was not the cause of the blindness.

   Jesus came, not to condemn, but to save. We should develop faith to perceive every evil as an opportunity for the works of God to be known. Yeshua was revealed as the Light of the world through this astounding healing. The windows of the man's soul had never been opened until that day of miracles.

   Jesus becomes whatever is needed in any situation as we exercise our faith. To the blind He is the Light of the world; to the thirsty He is Living Water; to the dying He is "the resurrection and the life."

2. Sin and sickness are closely related. The Lord will allow sickness and disease to come upon us because of unconfessed sin. I believe that First Corinthians 11:28-32 reveals that sickness, weakness, and even premature death are judgments resulting from carelessness or unconfessed sin. Sickness also results from eating the bread and drinking His cup in an unworthy manner, not discerning the Lord's body.

   "But let a man examine himself.... For this cause many are weak and sickly among you, and many [die.] For if we would judge ourselves we should not be judged" (1 Cor. 11:28,30-31).

   In Numbers 12, Miriam spoke against God's appointed leader, Moses. Thus, she touched God's anointed, and was saturated with leprosy for a season of repentance before she was restored. Praise the Lord that sickness can be removed when we make things right with the Lord. If you do not have a clear conscience but want to be healed, there is a remedy in First John 1:9 which states: "If we confess our sins, he is faithful and just to forgive us our sins, and to cleanse us from all unrighteousness."

Sometimes sin simply stands in the way. James offered the answer: "Confess your faults one to another, and pray one for another, that ye may be healed" (James 5:16). Perhaps you cannot think of any great sin that you have committed, yet, for all of us, our overall weakness is a fault we can confess. Sin is often the action resulting from weakness.

"...And the Lord shall raise him up..." (James 5:15). The Lord as restorer is truly divine healing—not the evangelist, not the elders, but the Lord Himself raises up the individual! Let us get our eyes off of doctors and anointed ministers, and onto the Lord!

A clue concerning sin and sickness is found in an ancient physician's oath attributed to the famous rabbi, Maimonides, which described sicknesses as messengers:

"...O God, Thou has formed the body of man with infinite goodness; Thou has united in him innumerable forces incessantly at work like so many instruments so as to preserve in its entirety this beautiful house containing his immortal soul, and these forces act with all the order, concord, and harmony imaginable. But if weakness or violent passion disturb this harmony, these forces act against one another and the body returns to the dust whence it came. Thou sendest then to man *Thy messengers,* the diseases which announce the approach of danger, and bid him prepare to *overcome* them"[1] (emphasis mine).

Indeed, sickness is often a wake-up call, but as the great rabbi, Maimonides, suggested, ailments are not insurmountable. If we will examine ourselves, repent, amend our ways, and appropriate the Lord's promises for health, we indeed will be overcomers!

3. Some sickness is a result of the violation of God's natural laws. These violations include poor eating habits, stress, failure to take proper rest, and lack of exercise. Twice in the New Testament we are informed that we are the temple of Yehovah and His Spirit dwells in us. Therefore, we should not abuse or defile the temple of God with contaminating substances, or God Himself will destroy our bodies. This major warning is found in First Corinthians 3:17: "If any man defile the temple of God, him shall God destroy…." Furthermore, Galatians 6:7 warns: "Be not deceived; God is not mocked; for whatever a man sows, that he will also reap" (NKJV).

Farmers poison our produce with many chemicals. Nutrients are removed in processing food; many toxic substances are added to our food. Our water is also tampered with in many places. Then we have the audacity to blame God and become embittered with the Almighty when sickness results! To walk in divine health, we cannot overlook the importance of dietary habits, as well as nutritional supplements.

4. Godly character cannot be neglected. Every major disease is usually associated with a deadly emotion at the root of the sickness. If we invite the Holy Spirit to remove the deadly emotion, which is like a poisoned dart, usually the body will heal itself. Our Creator has designed our bodies with powerful recuperative abilities. We know that stress is a cause of hypertension, but medical studies have also linked the deadly emotion of hostility with hypertension. Bitterness leads to burnout and degenerative diseases, although our bodies are designed to last for 120 years, according to Genesis 6:3. Deadly emotions can have further adverse consequences by leading to depletion of the immune function and thus triggering chronic allergies, fatigue, depression, environmental

illness, inflammation, decreased resistance to infections, fibromyalgia, cancer, and a host of other maladies.

5. Some sickness is due to the sins of doubt and unbelief. We believers rarely think that we are in a state of unbelief because, after all, we are *believers!* Yet let the truth be known: plenty of believers are filled with doubt and the sin of unbelief. You can hear unbelief in their conversations. What people say about themselves, their futures, and their bodies belies their status as believers. God works with words! As a matter of routine, "unbelieving believers" run off to doctors without consulting the Great Physician.

A lack of revelation concerning Jesus as Healer is perhaps the greatest hindrance to our healing. But when we have a real revelation that Jesus is Healer, that He came to do the will of the Father, that His stripes were the penalty and antidote for our sicknesses and diseases, then we can live as overcomers in that revelation. Even a negative report from a doctor should not elicit panic when we peacefully possess the revelation, "The Lord is my Healer."

Doubt and unbelief are often due to ignorance of the Word of God and the tenor of Scripture. During ministry time, I often ask people who come to me for prayer to recite a healing scripture. I do this to be sure they know assuredly that God wants them to be whole. They cannot be double-minded. They must have the evidence of God's Word to stand upon. Unfortunately, most of the time, people cannot think of a single healing scripture! Their ignorance of the Word of God and the many references to healing is appalling. However, when pressed, many will manage to quote from First Peter 2:24 (although the vast majority are not able to cite chapter and verse): "By [His] stripes [wounds] you were healed" (NKJV).

Let's examine the context of this oft-quoted verse:

> *For what glory is it, if, when ye be buffeted for your faults, ye shall take it patiently? but if, when ye do well, and suffer for*

*it, ye take it patiently, this is acceptable with God. For even
hereunto were ye called: because Christ also suffered for us,
leaving us an example, that ye should follow his steps: who
did no sin, neither was guile found in his mouth: who, when
he was reviled, reviled not again; when he suffered, he threat-
ened not; but committed himself to him that judgeth right-
eously: who his own self bare our sins in his own body on the
tree, that we, being dead to sins, should live unto righteousness: by whose stripes ye were healed* (1 Peter 2:20-24).

The context for receiving His healing stripes emphasizes
that we should be dead to sin and exhibit the Lord's character and qualities. Some casually assume, "Well, God will
just have mercy on me and heal me because I'm a believer,
and God is good." But can we continue to sin and still expect God to heal us? Please note the following points:

- The apostle Peter testified that guile was not found in
  the Lord's mouth. What is guile? It is defined as "insidi-
  ous cunning in attaining a goal; crafty or artful deception; duplicity."[2] Synonyms for guile include "trickery,
  fraud, craft."[3]

  Recently, a believer lied and acted in an underhanded
  way, which was observed by one of my coworkers,
  who commented: "This kind of behavior is typical of
  our currently 'sloppy agape' culture. May God forgive
  us that we can claim to love Him and yet miss the
  mark by sinning without even grieving."

- Jesus did not revile in return nor did He speak abu-
  sively.

- Jesus did not threaten when He was misunderstood.

- He committed himself to God who judges right-
  eously. There is great freedom in doing that!

Although salvation *is* by grace, we are nevertheless expected
to walk in a holy manner before God and to be as courte-
ous as possible, even when somebody offends us. Therefore,
character should be seen in the context of First Peter 2:24,

which states that we were healed by His stripes. Our continual mindset or goal should be to commit zero sin, and to maintain a clear conscience when we approach the Lord for healing—doubting nothing.

6. Jesus indicated that some people do not really want to be healed! They always make excuses. There was an invalid at the pool of Bethesda in Jerusalem who had suffered a deep-seated and lingering disorder for thirty-eight years.

> *When Jesus noticed him lying there [helpless], knowing that he had already been a long time in that condition, He said to him, Do you want to become well? [Are you really in earnest about getting well?]* (John 5:6 AMP).

The man started to make excuses but, in verse 8, Jesus simply said, "Get up!"

My father, of blessed memory, collected cute cartoons and jokes. One cartoon showed a woman sitting up in bed. In the background her husband was seen in the kitchen cooking and feeding the baby. A doctor attended by the woman's bed, earnestly saying, "You have to *want* to get well!" The expression on the woman's face was one of smug satisfaction. It was clear that she had no real intention of getting well!

Once I was taken to a woman's house to pray for her healing. She was wearing a beautiful bed jacket as she was propped up in bed, and painting her nails red on a hospital-style table. Neighbors bustled in and out with dishes of food. Her friend wanted me to pray the prayer of faith, but I could clearly see that the woman was enjoying the attention. She was certainly not desperate for any real prayer. Many others who receive disability allowances have no desire to be well and thereby forfeit those finances.

Jesus also tested the earnestness of blind Bartimaeus in Jericho. It is obvious to the reader that the blind man lacked his sight and should have wanted to be cured. Yet Jesus asked him pointedly, "What is it that you want from me?" (See Mark 10:51.) Jesus forced the blind man to ask specifically for his sight.

Does not James 4:2 state that "ye have not, because ye ask not"? So what do you really want Jesus to do for *you*? The answer may be very obvious to your family and friends, but **you** must also be specific and speak your genuine desire to be free from sickness. Dare to reach out to the Lord and vocalize your need. From Genesis to Revelation, our God is a Restorer and a healing God. One of the last scenes in the Bible, in Revelation 22:2, is the tree of life. Its leaves are for the healing of the nations.

7. Some people are not healed because Jesus and the Gospel offend them. The world would prefer to receive healing without getting right with God. The rebellious seek pseudo healings from the New Age, spiritualists, Eastern meditation, herbs, homeopathy, or fads, rather than from God's own prescription: the healing stripes of Jesus!

> *But he was wounded for our transgressions, he was bruised for our iniquities: the chastisement of our peace was upon him; and with his stripes we are healed* (Isaiah 53:5).

Jesus' timeless word is, "Be thou made whole!" When the Great Physician addressed a needy person, He commanded the person with, "Be thou made whole" or "Go in peace. Your faith has made you whole." Why was Jesus' *modus operandi* to speak words about peace and wholeness? Why those particular words?

Wholeness was His purpose on earth. "For the Son of man is come to seek and to save that which was lost" (Luke 19:10). In the beginning, you and I lost something. What did we lose? According to Genesis 1:27, "God created man in His own image" (NKJV). God's image is whole, unfractured; it certainly lacks nothing and is not diminished, sickly, sin-filled, diseased, weak, or broken. God is the epitome of wholeness. Wherever you are not whole, petition the Lord to fill in the gaps. Whatever part of your body is sick and shriveled, let Him breathe new life and resiliency into it. Whatever is empty, let Him fill it. Whatever is missing, let Him restore it!

8. Weakness and sickness occur also through perplexities and sorrows. In Charles Spurgeon's last sermon, he spoke of the power of perplexities, observing that a troubled spirit can deplete a person more than a month's labor. The mind can soon act upon the body, and the body fails sadly when spirits are bowed down with questions and fears. This, Spurgeon rightly said, is one reason why certain of our Lord's loyal-hearted ones are on the sick list, and must keep in the trenches for a while. The point, however, is not to stay on the sick list. There is a lifting in God when we snap out of the doldrums and once again join the ranks of believers!

Points to Ponder

1. How does sin impact healing? How does Scripture back this premise?

2. What effects result from ignorance of the tenor of Scripture? Has your life been impacted in this way?

3. If we truly desire to be healed, what emotional "needs" must we discard?

Notes

1. *The Menorah, a Monthly Magazine, Volume 3,* July to December 1887 (New York: Menorah Publishing Co., 1887), 388. http://books.google.com/books?id=k6QXAQAA-IAAJ&pg=PA388&dq=Thou+has+formed+the+body+of+man+with+infinite+goodness;+Thou+has+united+in+him+innumerable+forces&hl=en&sa=X&ei=M5txUuD0EojZsASjpYCQAQ&ved=0CEEQ6AEwAw#v=onepage&q=Thou%20has%20formed%20the%20body%20of%20man%20with%20infinite%20goodness%3B%20Thou%2

0has%20united%20in%20him%20innumerable%20forces
&f=false (accessed October 30, 2013).

2. Guile. Dictionary.com, *Dictionary.com Unabridged,* Random House, Inc., http://dictionary.reference.com/browse/guile (accessed: October 30, 2013).

3. Ibid.

Chapter 5

A HEALING TEST

We regularly and faithfully lay hands on the sick, sometimes with the anointing of oil. At other times, as led by the Spirit, we speak to mountains and give the word of command, even from a distance. Some are healed and some are not. Why? In the Bible, healing is God's stated will, but healing is promised to God's obedient children who do the will of the Father. There is also the issue of spiritual warfare, as well as the will and attitude of the sick person!

God's covenant of healing has conditions. In Exodus 15:26, God says: "If you will give earnest heed to the voice of the LORD your God, and do what is right in His sight, and give ear to His commandments, and keep all His statues, I will put none of the diseases on you which I have put on the Egyptians; for I, [Yehovah], am your healer" (NASB).

The following six probing questions may help you to be healed. This is not an exhaustive test, but the material does cover a lot of the bases and certainly addresses many issues.

1. *Is there any disobedience in my life?* In other words, have I obeyed everything the Lord has specifically told me to do? This important question is based upon Exodus 15:26 and its conditions. None of the diseases of the world are supposed to overtake God's obedient children, for "I, Yehovah, am your Physician." Sometimes people say they are no longer hearing from God, so I ask them, "What was the last thing God told you to do?" You may have to backtrack to

be sure you have completed all of God's instructions before you can clearly hear from Him again. Furthermore, according to Psalms 66:18, if we regard iniquity in our hearts, God simply will not hear us. This has to do with the theater of our minds. If we rehearse forbidden scenes, God will be far from us. "Regard" in this verse in Hebrew is *ra'ah*, which is to see, perceive, stare (look intently),[1] or envision. So if you are kissing your spouse but envisioning someone else, it is iniquity. Iniquity can be translated as "wickedness...evil, false, idol...mischief, mourners...sorrow,"[2] misfortune, or even trouble (which is the opposite of faith).

Are you indulging in any activity that the Bible condemns? These are important questions because of what Psalms 66:18 says: "If I regard iniquity in my heart, the Lord will not hear me...." Take a fresh look at the Ten Commandments. Are you breaking any of them? Are you cohabitating with somebody without the benefit of marriage? Are you engaging in sexual acts that the Bible defines as abominations? Are you dabbling in the occult? Do you traffic with demons by consulting psychic mediums? Are you stealing, coveting, or telling lies? After taking a spiritual inventory please note that Psalms 103 promises a marvelous benefit package for obedient believers: "Bless the LORD, O my soul: and all that is within me, bless his holy name....and forget not all his benefits...." The psalm lists benefits, but notice the order in verses 3 through 5: "Who forgives all your iniquities, who heals all your diseases, who redeems your life from destruction, who crowns you with lovingkindness and tender mercies, who satisfies your mouth with good things, so that your youth is renewed like the eagle's" (NKJV). The healing of diseases and the renewing of your youth are preceded by the forgiveness of your sins! When we get right with God, we can expect blessings, renewal of our youth and turning back of the clock!

Being in the Holy Land provides a point of contact that enables many healings. On every tour somebody is healed, to the glory of God. My Bulgarian friend Daniela was treated for cancer with chemotherapy, but God also gave her a special prescription—a *rhema* (living) word. He specifically instructed her to go and "dip" in the Jordan River to be healed! Now how many times have you heard of people dipping in the Jordan, or dipping into the waters of a shrine like Lourdes, and nothing happens? Nevertheless, it pays to obey God's specific instructions when we know the voice and promptings of the Holy Spirit!

In the Bible, Syria's General Naaman was instructed by the prophet Elisha to dip in the Jordan River seven times to be healed from leprosy (see 2 Kings 5). Naaman was insulted. He expected some other healing method from Elisha. At first Naaman refused. After all, Syria had its own river, so why did he need to dip in the Jordan? Likewise, my friend Daniela could have concluded, "God can heal me in my own country!" But she felt strongly that God had called her specifically to visit the Jordan River! As she continued to press into God for her healing, financial provision was provided for both herself and her husband to visit Israel. Daniela obeyed and dipped herself in the Jordan. Nothing seemed to happen. The symptoms were still there, but her husband's life was transformed by the trip to Israel, and when Daniela returned to Bulgaria, all of her medical tests came back negative—and the symptoms vanished. She had remained in faith by resisting thoughts and the devil's insinuations that she had "missed" God by going to Israel.

We invite you to go with us on one of our many healing tours to Israel. We do not guarantee that if you dip in the Jordan you will be healed, because there are no formulas in the healing ministry. But we do know that the Lord is present to heal both in your home nations and in Israel. Being in the Holy Land brings a special blessing that is hard to describe.

Again I ask, have you obeyed everything the Lord has instructed you to do? If the answer is "no," resolve outstanding issues with God so that your confidence toward God is not hindered.

2. *Have I forgiven everybody who has hurt, slighted, offended, or harmed me?* Most people simply have no idea how crucial this question is! The forgiveness issue must be faced regularly because offenses do come. Grudges are hazardous to health. You must be able to say with an honest and open heart, "Truly, I have forgiven even my enemies from my heart." Are you certain that you do not hold even a slight grudge? If you can truthfully say, "I have forgiven from my heart and I hold zero grudges," this is a very important step forward to be able to receive healing and to maintain health.

Why is forgiveness such an important principle in healing? Jesus taught in the forgiveness parable of Matthew 18 that we must forgive our enemies and those who persecute us. It is hard but not impossible. It is for our own benefit and health. The Lord told the parable about a man who was forgiven a colossal debt, yet this same man later refused to cancel somebody else's debt. The ingrate angered his master, and in Matthew 18:34, the master turned the man over to the tormentors. Who are the tormentors in life? Demons! Evil spirits! Notice the next verse: Jesus said: "My heavenly Father will also do the same to you [he will turn you over to the tormentors], if each of you does not forgive his brother from your heart" (Matt. 18:35 NASB).

This is heavy: Jesus clearly said if you cannot forgive, God also cannot forgive you and will consign you over to torturers. Physical sickness and mental disease are torment.

Therefore, to be free from physical and mental torment, we must purpose freely to forgive. Can you see that when we forgive our enemies, we outsmart the devil? Forgiveness is preventative medicine. When we forgive, we protect ourselves from being consumed with bitterness. When we forgive, we follow the example and lead of Jesus Himself. As He was being crucified, He said, "Father, forgive them; for they do not know what they are doing" (Luke 23:34 NASB). We must have a heart full of forgiveness.

A friend in Jerusalem was justifiably upset when his family's land was confiscated to build a security wall. I said, "Do you believe there is a God in heaven?" "Yes," he said, "I sleep at night because I do believe in justice." "Good," I said, "but you must outsmart the devil by forgiving your worst enemies, or God will turn you over to the tormentors." His face darkened, "How can I forgive them?" he asked, gritting his teeth. His religious background did not teach forgiveness. "You forgive," I said, "as a sheer act of your will without any emotion, as an act of obedience, because God tells us to release forgiveness for our own physical and emotional well-being." (This Arab was suffering from agonizing pains throughout his upper torso, but when he purposed to forgive his enemies, the pains subsided.)

Forgiveness frees us up psychologically rather than bottling up the poison of bile, bitterness, and hatred. God wrote our manufacturer's handbook, and so He knows exactly what He is doing when He requires His creatures to forgive.

Perhaps you are seeking healing from long-standing chronic pains or a serious disease. Jesus said that unless we forgive, our Father in heaven cannot forgive us! There are some things God Almighty cannot do, and one of them is to forgive somebody who refuses to forgive. So ask the Lord to show you any person you may need to forgive.

Speak forgiveness out loud as an act of obedience to God as soon as a name comes to your mind. Perhaps you need to forgive yourself for something. Go ahead and give yourself a break. Forgive yourself or anybody else, and then move on, light as a feather.

So, we have dealt with sin issues and obedience to God's instructions, as well as the vital issue of releasing forgiveness toward others. We have refused to hold a grudge. Now we can move on.

3. *Have I developed a genuine faith in God's promises by storing up the Word of God in my heart?* "Faith comes by hearing, and hearing by the Word of God" (Rom. 10:17 NKJV). If we are biblically illiterate, we cannot have a foundation for faith. The Word of God must dwell within us in order to be strong and to overcome infirmities. "Let the word of Christ dwell in you richly in all wisdom; teaching and admonishing one another in psalms and hymns and spiritual songs, singing with grace in your hearts to the Lord" (Col. 3:16). The Word must not be scanty but must dwell within our hearts in great abundance. This includes both Old and New Testaments, for the Lord is *The* Word and the Author of both. The Law of God must be written by faith upon our hearts. A little Word, little faith; much Word, great faith.

The following is an important healing passage about storing the Word: "My son, attend to my words; incline thine ear unto my sayings. Let them not depart from thine eyes; keep them in the midst of thine heart. For they are life unto those that find them, and health to all their flesh" (Prov. 4:20-22). Notice that the result of concentrating on the Word is health to the physical body (the flesh).

4. *Do I view unbelief as sin and as a dangerous enemy?* We do not hear very many people preaching on unbelief among believers. However, when we are "unbelieving believers," we exhibit toward God an "evil heart of unbelief, in departing from the living God" (Heb. 3:12). You may call yourself a

believer. You may attend worship services, but if you have an evil heart of unbelief, the Bible says you are backslidden. You are, in effect, an infidel. God's Word Translation renders Hebrews 3:12: "Be careful, brothers and sisters, that none of you ever develop a wicked, unbelieving heart that turns away from the living God."

When it comes to the healing message, by the stripes of Jesus, we *were* healed. He paid the terrible price for our healing at the whipping post and on the Cross, but do you really believe that? Or do you prefer to believe a doctor's report? Whose report do you really believe? Do you have, in effect, an evil heart of unbelief concerning the full price Jesus paid in the Atonement? Can you clearly see that unbelief is a much more serious issue than most followers of the Lord are willing to admit? Romans 14:23 states: "Anything that is not done in faith is sin" (GW). Can our faith come up to that standard?

We must not be "unbelieving believers." Faith comes by hearing the Word of God (see Rom. 10:17). Therefore, the only way we will protect the measure of faith that God has granted us is to make our faith grow by regularly meditating on God's Word and listening to healing scriptures—anointed teachers who reinforce the healing message in our spirits.

Faith is like a muscle. It must be exercised or it will atrophy. Iron also sharpens iron. Anybody can be healed by God's grace, mercy, anointing, and compassion at any time. However, keeping, maintaining or guarding our healing is another matter. Frequently my husband and I listen to one of our favorite healing teachers in order to sharpen our faith.

5. *Please answer, "True" or "False":* "I am healed because I feel like it." If you answered "True—I am healed because I feel healed," you have just become a sitting duck for the devil! If you are healed because you feel like it, what are you going to say when you don't feel like it? Will you say you

are not healed because you feel poorly? This question is related to the vital issue of maintaining your healing. Many receive a healing "on credit," but because they do not possess a real and abiding faith of their own, they often are unable to maintain their healing. This is because they believe or trust in recurring symptoms more than they believe the Word of God. The stubbornness of the devil to depart creates a real problem for people whose faith in God's healing promises is not fixed.

I will rephrase the statement: "True or False—I am healed because God's Word says I am healed!" If you answered "True," that means you have a good understanding of the rock-solid promises of God, who is a faith God. The Lord declares in Psalms 107:20: "He sent his word and healed them, and delivered them from their destructions." When we send a promise from God's Word into our situation, the Word accomplishes healing and delivers us. It does not return to us empty, but accomplishes the purpose for which it was sent: "[When My word] goes forth from My mouth; it shall not return to Me void [empty], but it shall accomplish what I please, and it shall prosper in the thing for which I sent it" (Isa. 55:11 NKJV).

This means that when you discover one of God's healing promises in the arsenal of His Word and declare it into your situation, His Word will work results, because the Word is living! God's promises in the Bible will not boomerang empty, but will produce healing and deliverance. God watches to see whether you remain in faith. When your faith has fully pleased Him, the healing is made manifest.

A famous preacher contracted tuberculosis in the days when there was no cure. While on his sickbed, somebody told him the good news of James 5:14-15: "Is any sick among you? let him call for the elders of the church; and let them pray over him, anointing him with oil in the name of the Lord: and the prayer of faith shall save the sick, and the Lord shall raise him up; and if he have committed sins, they shall be forgiven him."

The preacher believed this word, and called for the elders. He was anointed with oil, confessed his sins, and recovered. One day he was invited to preach again. He spoke for fifteen minutes, then a half hour, and finally, for a full, invigorating hour! He exclaimed, "Well, I do feel like I am healed!"

Do you hear any contradiction of God's Word in his statement? We are not healed because we feel like it. We are healed because God's Word says we are healed! If we do not learn this principle, the devil can sabotage our healing with recurring symptoms.

That is what happened with the preacher. He was ensnared by his words, which revealed that he was trusting in the lack of symptoms rather than God's immutable Word. The next morning, he woke up coughing blood.

"Lord, how did I lose my healing?" the preacher cried. The Lord replied, "You said you *felt* like you were healed. You did not confess your healing based upon My Word."

"Lord, I repent," the preacher said, "I am healed because Your Word says so." And immediately that man got up from his bed. He preached with vigor into his nineties.

I pray you have absorbed this lesson. Yet you often hear preachers make this unbiblical statement: "Sometimes God says 'yes'; sometimes God says 'no'; and sometimes God says 'maybe.'" Now is that an accurate saying? In truth, Second Corinthians 1:20 declares: "For all the promises of God in Him are Yes, and in Him Amen..." (NKJV). That means God says "Yes" to His obedient children every time, and our reply should be "Amen," in sync with God's Word!

6. *Do I actually believe it is God's will to heal me?* Very few people can say a definite "Yes" to this question because of the way they have been taught. Many sincerely want to believe

it is God's will to heal, but they are confused and not convinced, because they do not possess a confident knowledge of God's Word. Often they are ambivalent because of the various opinions of Bible teachers and theologians. But the Bible insists that "Even if everyone else is a liar, God is true" (Rom. 3:4 NLT).

So if you have a question mark in your mind concerning God's will to heal, you simply do not possess enough confident trust in His immutable Word to believe you will be healed! Uncertainty produces wavering. A harsh reality is Hebrews 11:6: "Without faith it is impossible to please [God]..." (NASB). (Yes, I repeat: not one person can please God without faith.) "...Whoever goes to God must believe that God exists and that he rewards those who seek him" (Heb. 11:6 GW).

In Mark chapter 1, God's willingness to heal is described beyond a shadow of doubt. Yeshua was sent to demonstrate God's will in the flesh, and never did anything contrary to His Father's will. A leper came to Him pleading, "Lord, I know You are able to heal me, but do You want to?" I love the way the Hebrew New Testament renders this verse! *"Ani rotze*—I want to!" The Lord forever answered the question, *Is it God's will to heal?* How did He answer? By stretching forth His hand, touching the leper (which made Jesus ceremonially unclean), and answering with warm affirmation, "I am willing! Be made whole!"

Because God has exalted His Word even above His name (see Ps. 138:2), His holy Word concerning the healing promises cannot be broken or denied when you meet its conditions. God's promises are guaranteed to bring results for His obedient children. If we will deny the "sloppy agape" distortion of the Gospel and keep the Lord's commandments, we can possess bold confidence toward God. "Beloved, if our heart condemn us not, then have we confidence toward God. And whatsoever we ask, we receive of him, because we keep his commandments, and do those things that are pleasing in his sight" (1 John 3:21-22).

7. *At what level am I in God's Word?* There are at least four stages of knowledge of God's Word. We are all climbing Jacob's Ladder. At which level are you?

   - Milk: "As newborn babes, desire the sincere milk of the word, that ye may grow thereby" (1 Pet. 2:2). Newborns are not yet skillful in handling God's Word but must begin to study the Scripture with unfeigned, pure hearts.

   - Meat: "Labour...for that meat which endureth unto everlasting life..." (John 6:27). At this stage of growth, you have a working knowledge of the Bible. But you must not stop here. "Study to shew thyself approved unto God, a workman that needeth not to be ashamed, rightly dividing [handling and teaching] the word of truth" (2 Tim. 2:15).

   - Strong Meat: This "...belongs to [the mature]...who by reason of use have their senses exercised to discern both good and evil" (Heb. 5:14 NKJV). At this level you have excellent discernment and are thoroughly grounded in God's Word. You should be adept at using the sword of the Spirit to ward off sickness and disease.

   - Oil and Honey: Men and women of God operating at this level possess certain revelations and truths that others have not pressed into God to obtain. At this level, the Holy Scriptures are "more precious than...pure gold; sweeter than honey..." (Ps. 19:10 NIV). "You have loved righteousness and hated wickedness; therefore God, your God, has set you above your companions by anointing you with the oil of joy" (Heb. 1:9 NIV). At this level your faith concerning the Atonement and all its benefits (including divine health) should be very strong.

May you increase daily in the knowledge of God's Word and earnestly reach for the healing that Yeshua sacrificially accomplished for you!

Points to Ponder

1. How can you apply the lesson of Daniela's testimony to your life?

2. How does forgiveness outsmart the devil?

3. What adjectives would you use to describe God's willingness to heal?

Notes

1. Biblesoft's New Exhaustive Strong's Numbers and Concordance with Expanded Greek-Hebrew Dictionary, CD-ROM, Biblesoft, Inc. and International Bible Translators, Inc. (1994, 2003, 2006) s.v. "ra'ah," (OT 7200).

2. Ibid., s.v. "aven," (OT 205).

Chapter 6

THE MYSTERY OF SUFFERING

Why do bad things happen to good people? Why does God allow the intense suffering caused by broken hearts, betrayals, natural disasters, accidents, murders, perversions, wars, carnage, and the deaths of loved ones? These questions are critical; they must be asked and answered. Because of heinous unspeakable sufferings such as the Holocaust, some people have abandoned their belief in God.

We must not shrug our shoulders and say things happen for no reason. Every one of us encounters problems, perplexities, and sorrows. We are often tested by grief, disappointments, even fear and sickness. But the prophet assured us that "He has borne our griefs and carried our sorrows..." (Isa. 53:4). When we call upon the Lord, the heavy burden is taken to the Cross. A book that has been very helpful in my spiritual walk is *Don't Waste Your Sorrows* by Paul Billheimer. The author points out that it is not the mere presence of suffering but how a believer reacts to suffering that determines spiritual growth in the midst of life's greatest adversities. Billheimer warns us not to waste our sorrows, but to harness disappointments and heartaches for the benefit of others.

One reason why troubles are allowed by God in our lives is to broaden our experience and make us more useful, compassionate people. If we have been too selfish and inward, troubles help us with insights that can help others. This is a reason why some people in the ministry seem to have had so many trials and tests. Widows can sympathize with widows. Those who have suffered poverty will show kindness to the poor. One who, by the grace of God has recovered from a terrible illness, will be empowered to help others to be healed. Sorrow is an opportunity to be used for the good of others.

I do not presume that we can answer to everybody's satisfaction the question of why God allows suffering. But I will tackle the question with some thoughts in harmony with God's Word.

Suffering: School of Surrender

The range of suffering is very broad, including mental and physical pains, agony, anguish, and emotional trauma. Suffering and the carrying of our individualized crosses are part of accomplishing exploits for God. If we strive to live godly lives, we will be ridiculed, misunderstood, and persecuted for speaking and living out the truth. Yet, in the midst of our sufferings, God draws near to us and proves Himself as "the God of all comfort" (2 Cor. 1:3).

Our world is governed by natural laws of cause and effect, sowing and reaping. If we violate any of these laws—if we eat too much junk food, or lose too much sleep, or become emotionally shattered over a period of time—we will suffer consequences. But what is difficult to handle is when we suffer because of external catastrophes or somebody else's foolishness, such as drunk driving, or the whole terrible topic of child abuse.

Suffering can be the result of breaking natural laws. It can be due to disobedience; or it can be, as the Bible teaches, caused by the opposition of evil spirits, even Satan himself. The late pastor David Wilkerson called suffering the "School of Surrender." Suffering gives us the opportunity to fall on our faces and cry out to God, saying, "I surrender all to You because I just can't handle this situation." And God's response is, "Good. I'll handle it. Your part is to *trust Me* completely."

When we suffer from sicknesses and disease, we can petition God for healing, because healing is part of the Gospel. But some of our sufferings are the result of events over which we have zero control. Therefore God allows sufferings to teach us to surrender with humility to His sovereignty.

The Job Account

In one of the oldest books in the Bible, we learn of a godly man who suffered greatly. As we read the Book of Job, the curtain is drawn back on spiritual realities and we see a drama: Satan, our great antagonist, is the culprit behind Job's suffering. It seems in some ways that the book was written to correct certain misconceptions about divine healing, and to reveal how actively Satan opposes believers.

The drama begins when the members of God's court and the Accuser, Satan, present themselves in Job chapter 1.

The Lord asks Satan, "Where have you come from?" The devil replies, "I have been patrolling the earth, watching everything."

Then the Lord asks Satan, "Have you noticed My servant Job? He is blameless—a man of complete integrity. He fears God and shuns evil."

Satan replies, "Yes, but Job has good reason to fear You, because You protect him. But take away everything he has, and he will surely curse You to Your face!"

The Lord answers, "You may test him by wiping out his possessions, but don't harm him physically." After Job endures terrible trials including the loss of his children, he still maintains his integrity. But Satan says to God, "This time if You strike his body, he will surely curse You to Your face."

Have you ever considered that the trial you are going through is because the Lord has boasted about you to the devil, the way He boasted about Job? The Lord who sees the end from the beginning knew in His omniscience that Job would stand up under trial. So God decreed, "Job is in your hands; only spare his life."

Satan afflicted Job with a miserable and painful skin disease. Job became careless with his speech in general but he never crossed the line to curse God, even though his wife urged him to "curse God, and die" (Job 2:9). In the end, God restored Job's health and blessed him twice as much as before. Satan, the accuser of the brethren, lost the challenge.

The Lesson of Job

What can we learn from Job's story?

First, we learn that satanic forces have an agenda. One element of that agenda is to entice people to curse God. God receives very bad press every day. Insurance companies describe natural disasters as "acts of God." Yet, many of the faithful defend His name!

Devouring us is also on Satan's agenda. We see in the Book of Job that Satan is often permitted to bring suffering upon the righteous. In Job's case, it looked as though Satan's devouring ways would succeed. But by the grace of God, suffering was used to perfect, establish, strengthen, and identify Job as God's child. The same is possible for all of God's faithful children!

The second lesson of Job is to avoid rash words in times of stress! The prologue and epilogue of the book reveal the source of Job's woes: it was malevolent, satanic opposition permitted by God to test Job. In between the story's beginning and ending is a lot of pious talk by Job's uncomforting "comforters." Job repented, saying, "I have heard of You by the hearing of the ear, but now my eye sees You. Therefore I...repent in dust and ashes" (Job 42:5-6 NKJV).

The text is clear: Job was not being punished for disobedience or gross sins. So, for what did he repent? His words! The famous preacher C.H. Spurgeon noted that Job repented for cursing his own birth, for his despair, for his desire to die, for all of his complaints against God, and also for his rash challenges of God.

The third lesson of Job is that life's sorrows empower us to minister to others. Bible scholars frequently point out that when Job prayed for his friends, the Lord turned his captivity around. Job's calamities were reversed!

Chastised, Not Punished

Although it is not a popular teaching, the Bible reveals that God also allows suffering to befall us as chastisement so we correct our ways. Suffering as chastisement was not the reason for Job's suffering, but it is nevertheless taught in both the Old and New Covenants. Chastisement is different from punishment. Chastisement has the connotation of our being disciplined with the hope that we will amend our ways. Punishment, in the strictest sense of the word, has a ring of finality, its purpose being to inflict a penalty.

It is fascinating that the Hebrew word for suffering is a plural noun, יסורים (or *yisurim* in its transliterated form), implying intensity. This word connotes not only tribulation, trials, and tests, but also chastisement and teaching. There is a purpose to suffering, a lesson to be learned that results in our spiritual growth. *Yisurim* also includes life's disappointments and the suffering caused by unfulfilled expectations. Chastisement as a consequence of sin is taught in both the Old and New Covenants. Let's look at Deuteronomy 8:5 in the Torah: "Thou shalt also consider in thine heart, that, as a man chasteneth his son, so the LORD thy God chasteneth thee." The Book of Proverbs—our book of daily wisdom (containing one chapter for each day of the month) also addresses chastisement: "My son, despise not the chastening of the Lord; neither be weary of his correction: for whom the Lord loveth he correcteth; even as a father the son in whom he delighteth" (Prov. 3:11-12).

This teaching of the Lord's correction is echoed in the New Testament: "… My son, despise not the chastening of the Lord, nor faint when thou art rebuked of him: for whom the Lord loveth he chasteneth, and scourgeth every son whom he receiveth. If ye endure chastening, God dealeth with you as with sons; for what son is he whom the father chasteneth not? But if ye be without chastisement…then you are [illegitimate children], and not sons" (Heb. 12:5-8).

Let's look at the last book in the New Testament, where the purpose of chastening is underscored again. In Revelation 3:19, the Lord says: "As many as I love, I rebuke and chasten: be zealous therefore, and repent." He does not enjoy correcting us, but chastisement is sometimes necessary to wake us up and shake us up! When we do not have the presence of mind to correct ourselves, the Lord lovingly chastises us, to keep us from straying. Suffering can be used to prevent us from being condemned and punished with the rest of the world.

Overview of Suffering

Now to sum up what we have noted so far. We saw *first of all* that suffering can be the result of violating laws of nature. *Second,* we learned that suffering can be caused by vicious spiritual attacks. This is spiritual warfare, a direct persecution from satanic forces. After all, the Bible says that Satan roams about like a roaring lion searching for vulnerable people to devour (see 1 Pet. 5:8).

Third, our suffering could be the discipline of the Lord Himself to address our rebellious sin or our shortcomings. His correction is always good. He is alarmed when we are headed in the wrong direction. He knows that if our actions are left unchecked, they could result in the damnation of our souls! Because God honors our free will, He will not stop us from sinning. But His Spirit will strive with us to amend our ways.

A fourth cause for some of our sufferings is God's pruning. Jesus used the analogy that He is the vine and we are His branches, directly connected to Him and to His life. In John 15:2, Jesus said that He would prune (cut) every branch. Any vineyard keeper will tell you that pruning helps the vine to bear more fruit. Naturally, the cutting is painful, but it is very necessary to the process of fruit-bearing. God is the gardener. He arranges painful circumstances, the elimination of individuals and situations from our lives, and even humiliating episodes that break us of pride and render us more useful. The greatest ministries of fruitfulness and comfort result from our greatest prunings and sufferings. These experiences give us the insight and brokenness to reach out compassionately to other suffering people.

There is a fifth category: it is voluntary suffering, or *cross-bearing.* Jesus said that as disciples who choose to follow Him, we must pick up our individualized crosses, and carry them. That is how we follow His example. We suffer when we are misunderstood or tempted, when we are treated with contempt, persecuted, avoided, imprisoned, disowned, physically beaten, or martyred like so many of our brethren in Africa, Asia, and the Islamic world. Please understand that this kind of suffering involves persecution and self-denial, not the bearing of sickness and disease. Jesus has already borne our physical pains, sicknesses, and diseases for us. "Pick up your cross and follow Me…" is a relational command. The vertical beam of the cross represents our developing an intimate relationship with the Lord, and being transformed into His image and likeness. The horizontal beam represents our relationships with others—loving when we are hated, blessing those who persecute us, dying to self, and making sacrifices.

A sixth reason for suffering is that it prevents us from loving this world too much. In this present life, we are in training for eternity. We are only pilgrims and sojourners here, because God has prepared a better world for us. Suffering develops in us the pilgrim mentality of a people passing through and not settling in for permanent residency. If there were no suffering in this life, would we be motivated to prepare for our eternal home?

The apostle Peter said suffering is like fire that purifies gold (see 1 Pet. 1:7). The apostle James said our trials produce maturity (see James 1:3-4), a maturity that we would not receive any other way.

A seventh reason: not only does suffering make us a more compassionate, sympathetic people, but hardships mold us into a praying people. We just do not learn to pray this way in easy-breezy times. The School of Suffering teaches us how to pray earnestly, with perseverance, and for the right things.

I know this firsthand, having moved into a new level of prayer when I was attacked physically and spiritually. Through the attacks on my health, I also became strong in divine healing.

Barren: Bad Luck or Bridge to Seek God?

The Jewish sages taught that nothing happens to us by random chance or luck. The secular concept of fate would say to a woman who cannot conceive children: "It's just bad luck that you were born with a barren womb. You must learn to live with it." But a Hebraic sense of destiny says, "God allowed this affliction, calling you to seek Him."

As we study the lives of barren women in the Bible, they sought God in their sufferings until they received power to conceive children. The trial of barrenness in the lives of Rachel and Hannah bore the fruit of special children. This was also true for Elizabeth, the mother of John the Baptist. The Bible teaches that even a woman who is never able to conceive can rejoice greatly in her spiritual children: "Sing, O barren one, who did not bear; break forth into singing and cry aloud, you who have not been in travail! For the children of the desolate one will be more than the children of her that is married, says the LORD" (Isa. 54:1 RSV).

If you are married, barren and want a child, we have faith to believe with you for a miracle baby! Many times we have seen God answer our prayers for couples to conceive children!

Our Supreme Example

As believers in Jesus, let us consider Him as our Master and supreme example. Isaiah 53:3 plainly predicted that His lot in life would be that of a Man of Sorrows, well acquainted with grief. Jesus told His disciples that the Son of Man must suffer many things; He would be rejected, even treated with contempt. Jesus' suffering was both spiritual (inward) and physical (outward). Think of just some of the sufferings He patiently endured: the humiliation of leaving realms of glory to be born in a lowly manger; a forty-day fast; the stigma of illegitimacy (only God and Mary were certain that she was a virgin); rejection by family and religious leaders. What's more, Jesus wept over Jerusalem, wanting to gather the city unto Himself as the Messiah. But the religious leaders rejected Him and, in time, He was betrayed. His own disciples did not understand Him most of the time. During agonizing prayer in the Garden of Gethsemane, He sweat great drops of blood; He was struck, spat upon, stripped, scourged, and crucified as a notorious blasphemer.

Our Yeshua's suffering was extreme, but Hebrews 2:10 declares that He was made perfect through the hardships. And, because He was tempted in all points, He is able to help us who are suffering and tempted.

Hebrews 5:8 also says that although He was a Son, Jesus (Yeshua) learned obedience through the afflictions and hardships that He endured. Can we expect better treatment than our Master? After all, a servant is not greater than his master, and the Lord plainly told us that we would be hated for His name's sake.

Paul's Suffering

Like Yeshua, the apostle Paul also graduated *summa cum laude* from the School of Suffering. Paul received a prophetic word in Acts 9:15-16 that he was a "chosen vessel unto me, to bear my name before the Gentiles, and kings, and the children of Israel…." Who wouldn't want to receive such a grandiose prophetic word? But wait—the prophecy continued: "for I will shew him how great things he must suffer for my name's sake."

So Paul was promised a glorious ministry, but he would also be called to endure great sufferings to fulfill his destiny. Indeed, he experienced a continual thorn in the flesh, literally "a messenger of Satan," as well as torture, mockery, malicious gossip, slander, and what he described in the Book of Romans as a "continual sorrow" because of the unbelief of his brethren, the Jews. At times he felt lonely, confused, and restless in his spirit.

Paul's thorn will no doubt be debated by theologians until we all get to heaven. Various commentators speculate that Paul's thorn in the flesh may have been:

(1) a bodily ailment of some kind;

(2) opposition encountered from his enemies, or suffering endured;

(3) carnal longings;

(4) spiritual trials, doubtings, etc.

Actually, Paul listed a catalogue of his afflictions in Second Corinthians 11, but it is very interesting to note that sickness and disease were *not* included in his list. Paul wrote: "Five times I received at the hands of the Jews the forty lashes less one" (ESV). (In other words, thirty-nine lashes in each of five beatings, equaling 195 lashes suffered by Paul.)

In addition, on three occasions, Paul was beaten with rods. One time he was stoned with rocks and left for dead, but miraculously stood to his feet and moved on to preach in the next town! Paul was also shipwrecked three times and spent a night and a day adrift at sea. Furthermore, during his frequent journeys he was in constant danger from robbers and from both Jewish and Gentile enemies determined to kill him. He toiled in hardships through many sleepless nights in hunger and thirst, often exposed to the cold. (See Second Corinthians 11.) In First Corinthians 15:31, Paul's motto was, "I die daily." *In his terrible list of sufferings, however, please note carefully that Paul did not once mention a chronic disease.*

Suffering as a Prize

The Early Church prized persecutions for the Lord as a privilege. The apostles rejoiced that they were counted worthy to suffer dishonor for the name of Jesus. How different is the average believer today! Do we consider it an honor when we are contradicted or humiliated? Or do we pout and become bitterly angry?

The apostle Peter said that Messiah suffered for us, leaving us an example to follow in His footsteps. The apostle James, the half brother of Jesus, advised us to count it all joy when we experience various trials (see James 1:2). Why? The testing of our faith and the fight of faith will produce steadfast character.

Both Paul and Peter were suffering apostles, and both were martyrs. Paul said in Romans 8:18 that he considered the hardships and sufferings of this present time insignificant compared with the glory that is to be revealed. Peter admonished us to rejoice when we share Messiah's sufferings because if we suffer with Him, we will also rule with Him (see 2 Tim. 2:11-12).

At this moment in history, Israel is suffering from anti-Semitism. We watchmen on Jerusalem's walls suffer along with Israel. To stand with the unpopular people of God will be increasingly difficult and controversial, demanding courage and suffering. *We must be careful that grief and suffering do not drag us down to sickness.* Continually we must appropriate this truth: "the joy of the LORD is your strength" (Neh. 8:10).

Sickness Is Not Suffering for God

There is a great difference between suffering for Messiah and for His causes and suffering because of the devil's sicknesses and diseases. We need to be able to differentiate between the two. *Provision has **not** been made in the Gospel to escape from suffering caused by persecution, but provision has been made for healing from pain and sickness in the Atonement.* Hallelu-Yah! This is why the Gospel is called Good News, because not only are our sins eternally forgiven, but also healing is available for our bodies— now, in this lifetime.

Divine health is the portion of all of God's obedient children. In Acts 10:38 the apostle Peter preached that Jesus was anointed and went about doing good and healing *all* who were oppressed by the devil. Jesus also taught in John 10:10 that Satan's agenda is to kill, steal, and destroy. But the Lord's agenda is to give us abundant life.

Part of the richness of life in Christ is explained in Paul's letter to the Philippians. He said that he wanted to know the Lord in "the power of his resurrection, and the fellowship of his sufferings" (Phil. 3:10). What is the fellowship of the Lord's sufferings? In short, I believe the fellowship of the Lord's sufferings includes sharing His heart for souls in a sin-sick world, for His persecuted brethren in the Suffering Church, for the perfection of His Bride, and also for the restoration of His people Israel.

While Yeshua ministered here on earth, though He never sinned, yet He became exasperated with His disciples' lack of faith. He exclaimed in Mark 9:19: "You unbelieving generation!…How long must I put up with you?…" (GW). I sometimes think I have an inkling of how He felt! Exasperation with the unbelief and lack of understanding of other believers is part of the fellowship of the Lord's sufferings! When He returns, will He find faith on the earth? (See Luke 18:8.)

Difficult Questions about Death

Death is the most difficult concept that we face. Why did a certain person die when he did? Why did God choose one person to live longer than the other? Why did another have to suffer before her death? The simple answer is that the Righteous Judge knows the bigger picture and sees better or more completely than we do.

Often we are asked, "Why the death of a loved one?" We do not always understand or have answers for why someone is taken by the Lord, or why prayers seemingly go unanswered. Concerning tragedies and what appears to be God's silence, we must bear in mind the great saying of Saint Paul, that we see in part, and know only in part (see 1 Cor. 13:12). All perplexities are solved in the light of absolute trust in God's all-knowing divine Love.

We have to let God's Word be true even when somebody dies and it looks as though our prayers were in vain. Many issues are involved when a sick person dies. There is no simple answer. Settle it firmly in your mind that your fervent prayers can never cancel another person's free will. Some of my friends were shaken in their faith because a family member for whom they had fervently prayed nevertheless died. They were about to lose their faith in divine healing, so I advised them, "Just because she died doesn't mean God's Word is not true. God always knows something about the situation, or some secret about the person's circumstances, that we don't know."

The authentic healer is sensitive to a sick person's emotions. When I am asked to pray for somebody, often I will sense a Holy Spirit-directed intuition to know if faith is actually resident in the person for healing. Sometimes we just know by the Spirit when it is a person's appointed time to die.

Often a friend or family member will have unrealistic expectations for miracles because they are not ready to face the departure of an elderly loved one. I visited a dying woman in the hospital who did not want to be healed even though her family and friends desperately wanted her to be restored. However, her strong desire was to go on to be with the Lord. Prayer for healing would have been futile and against the dying woman's wishes.

I enjoy connecting with people on Facebook and Twitter. Recently a woman wrote to me requesting prayer for a Christian gentleman seriously ill with cancer. She said the man, an author of inspirational books, was in his seventies, but she felt sure he had more work to do for the Lord. I replied, "The important thing is that *he* believes he has unfinished work to do. *He* must be willing to fight the fight of faith!"

A person's own attitude toward God as Healer is vitally important. I do pray that this man's spirit rises up in indignation against the cancer, and he fights the fight of faith. I also pray that he repents for any possible ground given to the evil one. That is not a judgmental statement—just a fact of life. We all need to examine ourselves from time to time, and especially when we are ill, to see if there is within us "an evil heart of unbelief," as Hebrews 3:12 warns. Disobedience can result in the consequences of sickness and disease.

Sin and Death

The intuitive healer may also perceive whether a person has committed a sin unto death. The Bible speaks of a category of such sin. Believers do not usually talk about this, but a sin unto death is a fact stated in the Bible, as First John 5:16 makes clear:

> *If you see a Christian brother or sister sinning in a way that does not lead to death, you should pray, and God will give that person life. But there is a sin that leads to death, and I am not saying you should pray for those who commit it* (NLT).

This verse teaches that sin should not be trifled with and no sin is trivial. There are various degrees and gradations in sin. There are sins of ignorance and there are deliberate, premeditated sins. There are sins of weakness such as Peter's, and also sins of betrayal, such as that of Judas.

I believe God sometimes takes an individual home to be with Him because He knows something about the future that would be soul-damaging had that person continued to live. He knows whether or not they would fall into sin or backslide. There are countless other reasons why death for some individuals is actually a severe mercy.

All sin leads to death (see Rom. 6:23) but some sins bring premature death. Only God knows if a person is sinning the aforementioned "sin that leads to death," meaning there is an unrepentant or long-standing issue (often not discernible by others) or an extraordinary mortal sin for which the apostle John discouraged futile petitions.

The "sin unto death" mentioned in First John 5:16 is not the unpardonable sin against the Holy Spirit committed by the hardened and malignant enemies of Messiah. In First John 5:16 the apostle clearly said that if one sees a brother (a fellow believer) sinning a sin unto death, he should not pray (or inquire) for the person to be healed.

Scholars say the verse refers to such a sin as God would chastise with disease and death. I knew a young man, for example, who heard the audible voice of the Lord when he was a teenager repeatedly calling him to serve in the ministry. He never answered the call and was struck down with a brain aneurysm. He died in his thirties.

A type of sin unto death was identified in First Corinthians 11:30, where Paul said weakness and sickness and even death were the results of taking the Lord's Supper in an unworthy manner. The comments of H. Bonar, D.D., in *The Biblical Illustrator* are helpful to understand this passage and how no sin should be considered trivial:

> How are we to know when a sin is unto death, and when it is not unto death, so that we may pray in faith? The last clause of the 16th verse answers this question. It admits that there is a sin unto death: which admission is thus put in the 17th verse: "All unrighteousness is sin; but all sin is not unto death."...If we cannot know when a sin is unto death, and when not, what is the use of saying, "I do not say that he shall pray for it"? The word translated "pray" means also "inquire," and is elsewhere translated so (John 1:19)....If thus rendered the meaning would be, "I say he is to ask no questions about that." That is to say, if he sees a brother sick and ready to die, he is not to say, Has he committed a sin unto death, or has he not? He is just to pray, letting alone all such inquiries, and leaving the matter in the hands of God, who,

in answer to prayer, will raise him up, if he have not committed the sin unto death.[1]

When somebody dies prematurely, God's reputation as Healer should never be impugned. Our position is James 5:14-16 which is clear, but with certain requirements (in bold type):

> *Is anyone among you sick? Then* **he [or she]** *must call for the elders of the church and they are to pray over him, anointing him with oil in the name of the Lord; and the prayer offered* **in faith** *will restore the one who is sick, and the Lord will raise him up, and* **if he has committed sins, they will be forgiven him.** *Therefore,* **confess** *your sins to one another, and pray for one another so that you may be healed. The effective prayer of a righteous man can accomplish much* (NASB).

So let God be proven true today in our lives even if everybody else is proven false!

God, Our True Judge

Upon hearing of the passing of another, we are taught in Israel to say, *"Baruch dayan emet,"* a Hebrew saying meaning, "Blessed is the True Judge." The essence of this statement is that all God does, He does for the good, and the implication of the saying is that God sees the bigger picture that we as mortals cannot possibly see! Indeed, the bottom line is, Father really *does* know best!

So even when it comes to death and tragedies, we are taught by our Jewish elders to have the presence of mind to bless God. When we say, "Blessed is the True Judge," we acknowledge that a death or tragedy is beyond our understanding. Our position should always be one of unquestioning humility before the Judge of all the earth: "Shall not the Judge of all the earth do right?" (Gen. 18:25).

The rabbis teach that, because there is an infinite difference between us and God, it is not always possible for us to understand His mysterious ways. We might not comprehend, yet despite the pain of bereavement, we acknowledge the following: the True Judge knows what He is doing; He is good; and He is in control of our lives.

Too often, we lose sight of God's goodness and instead display symptoms of a character "disease": *blaming God*. This is a serious issue. It is disturbing to see people shaking their fists at God. When we read the Book of Job, for example, we know that Satan afflicted Job with many sorrows and calamities. Yet Job never once sinned by charging God "foolishly" (see Job 1:22).

How many times have we charged God foolishly in a situation? God is just and holy. Instead of murmuring and complaining against Him when things go wrong, we should carefully examine ourselves. It is far more likely that the root of the problem is sin or rebellion (ours or other people's), none of which issues forth from God's throne.

Wisdom of the Kaddish

The Jewish prayer, the *Kaddish*, helps us to keep a positive and dignified attitude toward death. Literally meaning "sanctification," the *Kaddish* is a prayer with emphasis upon God rather than our feelings, emotions, doubts, or misgivings. Traditionally, the *Mourner's Kaddish* is said for a deceased relative or closest kin (parent, sibling, spouse, or child). It is a short prayer that, in fact, does not mention death at all!

In the Jewish world it is customary to honor a relative's memory with special services on the first anniversary of their passing. In the continuity of the ages, our brethren in the Eastern Orthodox Church also follow this therapeutic practice.

I asked my Orthodox Jewish friend, Gidon Ariel, why the *Kaddish* is associated with death and the passing away of loved ones. Gidon said the answer is clear: "If a person who has experienced a tremendous loss is able to express his trust and faith in God that a great cosmic plan exists and all tragedies are a part of His great plan, then there is no greater sanctification of His great name than this. Since the *Kaddish* is said publicly, this strengthens faith in God on both a personal and community level."

I believe the Kaddish is a wonderful concept and catharsis. Jesus made a deeply profound statement in John 4:22, saying, "salvation is from the Jews" (NIV). Indeed, our debt to the Jewish people for the Torah and Messiah cannot be calculated or fathomed. Having prayed often for the sick and dying, I have noticed (even among real believers within the Church) a questioning and sometimes even anger at the Almighty when someone dies prematurely or even in old age. The Jewish method of mourning has a maturity that could teach us much about attitude and "closure."

Unfortunately, the Church's tragic disengagement from the Jews through the centuries has robbed us of the richness of the sap and dignity of our Hebraic roots. We can reclaim them! Here is the beautiful, spiritually elevating, and full-of-faith *Kaddish*. I believe we can all say "Amen" as we read it:

> *May God's name be made great and sanctified. Amen. In the world that He created according to His will, in His kingdom in which He reigns supreme, may His salvation sprout forth and may His Messiah be close, in your lifetime, and in the lives of all Israel, speedily in our days. Say Amen. Amen. May His great name be blessed forever and ever. May the name of the Holy One, blessed be He, be blessed, praised, extolled, raised high, and made great—Blessed be He!—higher than all blessing or song, praise or consolation. Say Amen. May great peace from heaven and good life be ours and upon all of Israel. Say Amen. May He who makes peace in His heights make peace upon us and upon all Israel, and say Amen.*

Hope in a Fallen World

Every family suffers many things because we are living in a fallen world and in the general time that the Bible calls the "birth pangs of Messiah." Grief, bitterness, and despair are like weeds in a garden in summertime; we must keep rooting them out until the season changes!

I want to invite you to trust the Lord in the things you are suffering, and to know that He will work out all things for good for those who love Him and who are called according to His purposes (see Rom. 8:28). All of us eventually experience the death of a loved one. Many suffer the agony of a crushing divorce. If you are hurting from the deep pain of loss, you might be among those who are angry with God. If you are suffering from sickness and disease, the very Good News is that healing is available in the Gospel, if you will humble yourself and ask the Lord to heal you.

Some reading this book have not yet begun a close relationship with Jesus. Now is the time to start. If you have a broken heart, if you are suffering in any way, or if you want to connect with the Lord, I invite you to pray to Father God, because we all need Him sooner rather than later.

Meanwhile, I pray this prayer on behalf of all who are suffering:

> *Gracious Abba Father, people are suffering. I believe that You are the God of love, the God of compassion. Wrap Your arms around those who are suffering, including the reader. Enfold them in Your love.*
>
> *Relieve our suffering and give us eyes to see how we can help to relieve the sufferings of others. We thank You that healing is part and parcel of the Atonement, and we ask for a supernatural touch now in the name of Yeshua, Jesus the Messiah. Amen.*

Points to Ponder

1. Name two "ingredients" essential to our accomplishing exploits for God. How and why does anti-Semitism cause suffering among Christian believers as well as Jewish?

2. Describe the difference between chastisement and punishment, in your own words. How does the distinction affect your understanding of trials?

3. Have you ever suffered from the character "disease" of blaming God? Was He really to blame for your loss? Why or why not?

Note

1. Joseph S. Exell, *The Biblical Illustrator, New Testament Volumes,* electronic database (Ages Software and Biblesoft, Inc., 2006).

Chapter 7

DEALING WITH DEMONS IN THE TWENTY-FIRST CENTURY

There was a lunatic boy mentioned in the Gospels. His father brought him to Jesus' disciples, but they failed to heal the boy. Embarrassed by their failure, the disciples came privately to Jesus, asking, "Why couldn't we cast out the demon?" Jesus' answer still applies today: "Because of your little faith" (Matt. 17:20 ESV). Jesus added that more prayer and fasting were also required.

Difficult cases should inspire us to increase our faith. The disciples were perplexed because Jesus had already given them power and authority to heal and to cast out devils. In Luke 10 they enjoyed a certain measure of success. Jesus sent them out two by two, and when they returned, they rejoiced that even devils were subject to them.

That is, until this humiliating encounter.

Demons Are Real

Today's "unbelieving believers" no longer ask the Lord, "Why couldn't we drive out a demon?" Most professing believers will not even acknowledge that demons are real! The debate continues over the subject, with questions such as "Can a Christian have a demon?" (The reality is that a true born-again believer cannot be demon-possessed; but he or she can be oppressed. We can be attacked by dark spirits if we don't know how to resist and engage in spiritual warfare.)

Jesus' disciples knew demonic activity was real, and often related to physical and mental ailments. Some manuscripts render their question in Matthew 17:19: "Why could we not heal him?" This rendering poses a classic case of "what comes first, the chicken or the egg?" In some situations, healing cannot manifest until a demon is discerned and cast out.

When the boy's father told Jesus, "I asked Your disciples to drive out the spirit, but they couldn't" (see Matt. 17:16), Jesus' response, reflected His sorrow and exasperation: "You unbelieving generation! How long must I stay and put up with you?" (see Matt. 17:17). Jesus had continually worked miracles in their midst, yet they remained unbelieving. (The Lord must have been thinking: "Am I the only one who can deal with this? My disciples still aren't up to speed!")

Jesus said a perverse generation does not know how to deal with demons! Think about that! Although the people were perverse and Messiah was clearly provoked, He was faithful to take care of the child: "Bring the boy to Me," Jesus said. That is exactly what all parents should do when their children have needs!

When the spirit saw Jesus, it immediately threw the boy into a violent convulsion, foaming at the mouth, and rolling on the ground. This misery had been going on from the boy's childhood. No wonder the father begged Jesus: "If You can do anything, take pity and help us."

But begging prayers do not get the job done. Faith does.

In Mark 9:23, Jesus turned the question on the father, essentially saying, "If I can? You mean, if *you* can. All things are possible to him who believes!"

The father cried, "I do believe! Help my unbelief!" (See Mark 9:24.) His reply was transparent, but it revealed double-mindedness.

Meanwhile, a crowd gathered, and the demon put on a display. Demons crave attention, which is a form of worship for them. But Jesus soundly rebuked and nailed the spirit, specifically commanding a deaf and mute spirit to come out. This was a demonstration of the gift of discerning of spirits. The demon shrieked, convulsed the boy, causing him to collapse in a heap that resembled a corpse.

What a scene! We have witnessed similar scenes over the years. After being tormented by a demon, a woman in one of our meetings in Cairo collapsed. She also appeared to be dead, but we commanded her in the name of Jesus to get up. She did, to God's glory. We saw this tactic of the devil again, in one of our open-air meetings in Pakistan. A woman in the crowd appeared to be playing dead. In the name of Jesus, we rebuked the spirit of death and she was set free.

Sometimes, when this happens, the eyes of seemingly dead people roll up in the back of their heads so that only the whites of their eyes are visible. This is an evil spirit's way to avoid looking at you and to keep the victim from making contact and receiving help. Take immediate authority, in Yeshua's name!

In the Bible scene, people assumed the boy had died. But Jesus lifted him by his hand, and the boy stood up on his feet. When the disciples approached Jesus privately, He assured them that they had *not* lost the power to do miracles. He said, "If you have faith as a grain of mustard seed [the least of all seeds], you can remove mountains. And nothing will be impossible for you" (see Matt. 17:20).

The borders of our faith should reach to where "nothing is impossible" because of our trust in God's greatness! The tiny mustard seed should encourage us: we do not have to be faith giants, but we do need to start exercising our faith in God!

Enemy No. 1: Unbelief

Our worst enemy is unbelief. God expects us to believe His promises and to *act*. I like the name, The Book of *Acts*. Thank God it is not the "Book of Apathy," but the "Book of Action." The title comes from a Greek word used in early Christian literature to describe the exploits of the key apostles and disciples in the decades following the Lord's ascension.

Faith and trust in God separates "the men from the boys."

Biblical faith gives you the determination and power to resist the advice of unbelieving family members and well-meaning friends;

otherwise they would drive you over the cliff of unbelief. Unless you pay them no heed, they will push you to go to the doctor or hospital because of *their* fears and unbelief. They will insist that you have medical tests.

I praise God for medical advances that have helped many people. For example, a bionic eye has been invented in Israel! But at the same time, don't neglect to develop biblical faith! Medical tests often stir up and strengthen devils, and can open the door for sickness to gain a foothold in your body through a diagnosis (rather than taking your case to the Lord our Healer). In countries such as the United States, where sicknesses are regularly advertised on TV, it can be difficult to maintain a biblical faith in God. In nations such as Britain and Israel, where medicine is socialized, the Lord our Healer is often not the first choice, even in the minds of "believers."

Authority over Demons

When was the last time you heard somebody rebuke a demon? In Matthew 17:18, Jesus rebuked the devil. Sadly, many people in the Church today do not even think to rebuke evil spirits, because they are not trained to act biblically and their minds are conditioned by governmental health services and advertising to depend upon medicines.

The Church has apostatized to the point that most unbelieving believers laugh cynically when demons are mentioned! Priests who exorcise devils are stereotyped by central casting as fanatics. I heard a Baptist deacon say, "Do you know how long it took me to learn to rebuke the devil?" The thought had never crossed his mind to cast out a demon, because his Baptist church never discussed such matters. But as the deacon studied the Bible, it became clear that Jesus gave His followers power to rebuke and to cast out evil spirits; so the deacon began to take authority over demons, with great success.

Jesus cited two reasons for His disciples' failure to heal the boy in Matthew 17. Number one was their unbelief, or literally, their "little faith." Second, Jesus taught a harsh reality: that stubborn spirits are cast out because of a believer's consecration to God by devoting extra time and energy to fasting and prayer. A casual believer who has never added fasting to his prayers is not a likely candidate to get the job done.

Some evil spirits are more wicked and obstinate, and they are not easily evicted after a long tenure. In Matthew 12:43-45, Jesus said: "When an unclean spirit goes out of a man, he goes through dry places, seeking rest, and finds none. Then he says, 'I will return to my house from which I came.' And when he comes, he finds it empty, swept, and put in order. Then he goes and takes with him seven other spirits more wicked than himself, and they enter and dwell there; and the last state of that man is worse than the first…" (NKJV).

Although all things are possible, some works are more difficult to accomplish than others. The disciples learned that the exorcist needs special preparation. Fasting subdues the flesh, and increases the spirit of revelation. By means of prayer and fasting, a believer can invest into the banks of fasting and prayer to receive greater power to withstand assaults of the evil one.

The word translated *lunatic* in *The King James Version* of Matthew 17:15, is taken from a Greek word meaning to be "moon-struck"[1] (supposedly influenced by the moon's movements, although some translations render this word as *epileptic*).

Let's look at this whole topic from another angle. Today the word *lunatic* means someone who is mentally ill. No doubt, the boy in the Gospel appeared to be deranged. Mental illness was and is a problem in our world. Today stress, uncertainty, and the side effects of high-powered drugs can cause people to go crazy and commit suicide or murder.

A man wrote to a rabbi that he felt depressed and worthless because of a serious mental illness. How many people feel exactly like that! The man bemoaned his failures, despairing that all his old school friends appeared to be successful. He ended his letter asking woefully, "What am I worth?"

The rabbi gave a compassionate response: "First of all, we must understand man's purpose on earth. Is it to be a Torah scholar? Is it to be admired by everybody? Is our purpose to have a high status in life? No! Man's purpose is to serve God." The rabbi said we were created "for the sole purpose of rejoicing in God and deriving pleasure from the splendor of His presence." This brings to mind the Westminster Catechism that I learned from my father, a Presbyterian minister, of blessed memory. The first question of the Westminster Shorter Catechism asks, "What is the chief end [or purpose] of man?" The catechism's answer is: "Man's chief end is to glorify God and to enjoy him forever."[2]

Amen!

The Master of the Universe is not an achievement-oriented elitist. In the world to come, there will be many surprises. People considered important and celebrated here on earth will be considered worthless in the world to come, and many who are derided here will be highly important there. "Do your best," the rabbi advised, "and always be aware that you are precious in G-d's sight."

"Do your best" is certainly wise advice on a certain level of understanding. However, in this Gospel Age, we are expected to believe God's promises of health and guidance. We are expected to know how to rebuke evil spirits and to cast them out. Jesus expected us to fast and pray to be able to give the word of command to relieve the oppressed and possessed. Dealing with demons is surely part of the Great Commission: "And these signs will accompany those who believe: in my name they will drive out demons..." (Mark 16:17 NIV).

Carrying on Jesus' Ministry

Deliverance from evil spirits is part of the Gospel! Many times, if you are a discerning believer, you can see the presence of evil or evil intent in somebody's eyes. Truly, eyes are the windows of the soul.

The ministry of exorcism, or casting out devils, is an important work of the Holy Spirit. Yet, due largely to sensational movies and unbalanced teachings, there remains much misunderstanding, and even ridicule of this aspect of the ongoing ministry of Jesus the Messiah. We must have a balanced view of this legitimate and needful biblical ministry. After all, Jesus' ministry consisted of four main activities: prayer, teaching, healing, and casting out demons.

For many years as part of our healing outreaches we have prayed for people who need healing and deliverance. Because my husband and I were also part of an outstanding ministry in Africa, we have seen many people bound by witchcraft set free in the name of Jesus. I will never forget praying for a madman who wandered into one of Reinhard Bonnke's meetings in Africa. In the name of Jesus, he was restored into his right mind.

But the casting out of demons is not just a ministry for Third World countries. With apostasy in Western churches and so many people everywhere trafficking in the occult, deliverance ministry is vital worldwide.

When we first joined Reinhard Bonnke's team in Africa, we noticed in his big outdoor meetings that there were "deliverance" tents for ministry. In the beginning, we asked if the ministers in the deliverance tents were especially qualified to do this work. But the person in charge said, "Casting out demons is the work of *every* believer according to the Great Commission!"

Indeed, in Mark 16:17-18 the first of five signs that are supposed to follow every believer are clear: We are to "cast out devils," "speak with new tongues," and "take up serpents." If we "drink any deadly thing," it will not hurt us. We will also "lay hands on the sick, and they shall recover."

So casting out, or exorcising demons, is among the primary duties of every disciple of Jesus! But how few actually do it!

Discerning of Spirits

Although it is the duty of every disciple to continue the works of Jesus—and that surely includes casting out demons—we also must heed the admonition of the apostle Paul to covet spiritual gifts. The discerning of spirits mentioned in First Corinthians 12:10 is especially important; through it we can know whether someone is influenced by the Holy Spirit, the natural human spirit, or an evil spirit. Using this God-given gift, some believers can even discern the identity or name of the particular evil spirit(s) (lust, murder, greed, and so forth).

Leaders in the deliverance ministry sense the presence of evil spirits in different ways: perhaps they experience chills, or an unease in their spirits. Sometimes they perceive a foul odor. When Saint Catherine of Siena visited the pope's court, she was overwhelmed by a stench that she attributed to sin and demons, rather than to natural causes.

I have also experienced these manifestations. The Lord works with us, providing such words of knowledge. He does not expect us to grope in the dark. With Him, we can become finely tuned to detect evil, just as a smoke detector recognizes fire.

Unfortunately, as we draw closer to the Second Coming of Jesus, there is an alarming decrease in overall discernment in the Church. Many people are not able to endure sound doctrine and biblical preaching, but are instead listening to fables and succumbing to doctrines of demons (see 2 Tim. 4:3; 1 Tim. 4:1). We should arm ourselves with a great knowledge of the Word of God in light of the fact that Jesus warned us that deception would be a primary characteristic of the Last Days.

There are many categories of evil spirits that we should be able to discern, such as New Age spirits and spirits of the occult.

For example, familiar spirits are just that—they are familiar and acquainted with our past and family background. Familiar spirits take on many guises and masquerade, for example, as departed relatives.

The Bible sternly warns against dabbling in the occult. In the Torah, for example, is this prohibition in Deuteronomy 18:10-11: "There shall not be found among you anyone who makes his son or his daughter pass through the fire, one who uses divination, one who practices witchcraft, or one who interprets omens, or a sorcerer, or one who casts a spell, or a medium, or spiritist, or one who calls up the dead" (NASB). The next verse says: "For whoever does these things is detestable to the Lord..." (Deut. 18:12 NASB). Notice that these practices are absolutely detestable to God!

Don't Be Deceived!

A number of TV shows promote trafficking with familiar spirits. Some do so by preying upon gullible souls who desire to contact deceased loved ones. But it is not possible to contact the dead; God has fixed a gulf between the dead and the living, according to Luke 16:26. Therefore, spirit voices and visions impersonating the dead are deception—*big time*. There is nothing so untrustworthy as demonic deception! Here is something else very important to know and to learn: Demonic powers can appear to heal people simply by withdrawing the evil they (the demons) inflicted in the first place. Consequently, people are duped into believing that they have been healed by witchdoctors, shamans, or New Age practitioners. This is why so many false ministers seem to be able to heal and to hook their victims with lying wonders. It is very important to understand that satanic forces can remove their oppression with the express intent to deceive people into trusting false healers.

Jesus commanded devils to depart, and we should do the same in His name. I usually say to a demonic presence with great authority: "Be gone from me in the name of Jesus!" When evil spirits recognize your authority in Jesus, I guarantee you, they will depart. But if demons have gained a legal foothold in your life due to sin, you will have an ongoing battle on your hands until the sin is renounced and repentance is done.

The Devil Correctly Viewed

Some Christian circles place too much emphasis on the devil. I will never forget mentioning to evangelist Reinhard Bonnke some years ago a communication I had read about voodoo priests in Haiti. The priests were planning to sacrifice a goat on a mountain, in order to rededicate Haiti to the devil. "Reinhard!" I said, "We need to pray!"

His answer was dismissive. He was not impressed with the devil's power. Reinhard Bonnke is totally impressed with the power of the blood of Jesus. He said, "Oh, Christine, don't you know the Lord dealt with all of that hocus-pocus 2,000 years ago at the Cross?"

Well, amen! I learned to take his attitude on board! Once, after a meeting, a woman begged Reinhard Bonnke: "Pastor, help me!"

"What's wrong?" Reinhard asked.

The woman told him she was troubled by a demon sitting on her shoulder. In a flash, the right answer came to him: "Lady, flies only land on cold stoves!"

Amen! If the fire of God is in you, no fly, or devil, will sit on you for very long!

So in *Exploits Ministry*, we do not overemphasize the power of the demonic realm. We do, however, need to caution believers in these Last Days that Satan is desperate. He realizes that his time is drawing short, and he is patrolling the earth as a roaring lion seeking whom he may devour. Let's be ready and know how to resist him!

Supernatural Protection

Not only do we possess the protection of the Ephesians 6 armor of God, but also the prayer Jesus taught us to pray: The Lord's Prayer (see Matt. 6). The prayer includes the request, "deliver us from evil" (Matt. 6:13). The accurate translation of the *New International Version* is "deliver us from the evil one," meaning Satan. "Deliver us from evil" should be a frequent prayer in this increasingly dangerous world. Jesus knew full well that there are demons, and He taught His disciples to subjugate them. The trouble is that many institutional Christians are too sophisticated, jaded, and skeptical to address this subject with anything but scorn. They do not really know the Master.

When I was ministering in the revival in Arabia, I was told that a Christian leader had died because someone cursed him with sickness. I explained that this kind of mentality does not belong to a strong believer. The Bible declares in Proverbs 26:2 that an undeserved curse does not alight—it simply cannot stick to an obedient child of God.

You *cannot* curse what God has blessed. If you are a strong, obedient believer, any curses, hexes, or spells hurled at you are null and void in the name of Jesus. If any evil spirits have been sent on assignment against you, in the name of Jesus, you have the power and the authority to decommission them.

Avoid These Pitfalls

Nevertheless, the late Bible teacher Derek Prince, of blessed memory, whom we knew in Jerusalem and admired, taught four primary categories of sin that would ordinarily call down a curse upon a person:

- Worship of false gods—This includes involvement in the occult or witchcraft (see Deut. 18:10-12).

- Disrespect for parents—This shortens life (whereas honoring parents leads to a long life, according to Exodus 20:12).

- Oppressing people, especially the weak—Derek mentioned that abortion, for example, ordinarily brings a curse.

- Illicit or unnatural sex.

I would also add the following:

- Unforgiveness, bitterness, or resentment—Jesus warned that unforgiveness turns us over to the tormentors.

- Speaking evil of, or causing harm to, God's ministers—This refers to touching God's anointed (see 1 Sam. 26:9).

- Disregard or disrespect for the Jewish people—Anti-Semitism brings the curse of God according to Genesis 12:3, where the Lord declares: "And I will bless those who bless you, and the one who curses you I will curse. And in you all the families of the earth will be blessed" (NASB).

Setting Spiritual Issues Right

Through prayer we can come to God and ask Him to forgive us. We can also ask Him to *deliver* us, if necessary! A sure and wonderful promise that I have relied upon many times is First John 1:9: "If we confess our sins, he is faithful and just to forgive us our sins, and to cleanse us from all unrighteousness." In Psalms 50:15, we also have this marvelous promise: "Call upon Me in the day of trouble; I will deliver you, and you shall glorify Me" (NKJV). It is amazing: when we are living holy and righteous lives, the evil one cannot touch us. I like *The New Living Translation's* rendering of this truth: "We know that God's children do not make a practice of sinning, for God's Son holds them securely, and the evil one cannot touch them" (1 John 5:18 NLT).

But if we have opened the door to Satan and have said, in effect, "Come right in," whether through sin or disobedience, we must take action to remove any consequential curses. If Satan has gotten his foot in our door, he must be evicted in Jesus' name. So when Satan knocks, let Jesus answer the door!

First we must repent, confessing our foolishness to God. Second, we must renounce what we have done. To renounce the sin is different from repenting. Repentance involves turning to God, admitting our guilt, and asking Him to forgive us. Renunciation involves turning away from wrong activity and taking a permanent stand against evil.

Having done these two things—repentance and renunciation—we can be freed from any curse. (It is helpful to voice these steps to another believer as a witness and prayer partner.)

Occultic "Invitations"

What about owning and or *displaying occult objects in your home?* Reinhard Bonnke always taught this truth in his Gospel campaigns: if you have idols, charms, witchcraft potions, or any of the devil's paraphernalia in your home, Satan has the right to visit and inspect his property.

This teaching is in line with the Bible. In Acts 19 the apostle Paul ministered powerfully in Ephesus in the Roman province of Asia Minor. A solemn fear descended on Ephesus, and Jesus' name was greatly honored. Some who had practiced magic burned their books in a public bonfire. The value of the books was great, but these people were wise to burn the devil's property. They would rather be finished with sin rather than resell the books and cause others to stumble. A person to whom I was ministering rejected this truth. He could not be set free because he flatly refused to destroy his collection of expensive Asian idols from trips to the Far East. He cared more about the artifacts and the money he had spent than his personal health and standing with God.

Once your house is free from accursed books and DVDs, decorations, and other questionable objects, a great peace will shine in your home.

Be mindful also of gifts from others. On some of our ministry trips members of our team have been given trinkets. Upon closer examination, they realized they could not keep some of them, because they were accursed objects associated with demonic powers and symbols.

Deliverance for the Oppressed

It is a common question: Can a Christian be possessed by a demon?

We are created as three-part beings: we have a spirit and a soul, and we live in a body. When we receive Jesus' Atonement and are born again, the Holy Spirit takes up residence in our spirit. Therefore, the spirit of a born-again believer cannot be possessed by devils. Nevertheless, we can still battle fleshly and soulish desires under the influence of evil spirits which must be resisted and commanded to leave. How do you minister deliverance to those who are oppressed in this way? Just lead them to renounce evil and to sever themselves from generational curses, because the sins of the fathers are transmitted down to the third and fourth generations (see Exod. 34:7). We must renounce and take authority over any known or unknown generational curse, including family involvements in secret and occult societies such as Freemasonry.

Deliverance is also for the physically ill, as we have already seen. Remember that oil is a symbol representing the Holy Spirit. In James 5:14-15 in the New Covenant we read:

> *Is any sick among you? let him call for the elders of the church; and let them pray over him, anointing him with oil in the name of the Lord: and the prayer of faith shall save the sick, and the Lord shall raise him up; and if he have committed sins, they shall be forgiven him.*

So it is the name, Yeshua, Jesus the Anointed One, accompanied by the anointing with oil and the prayer of faith that brings healing and deliverance. According to James, this anointing is done by the leaders, the elders of the church.

You might say, "Well, I'm a believer, but I'm not an elder." There is another type of anointing with oil; some ministers refer to it as "evangelistic anointing." Evangelistic anointing with oil was recorded in Mark 6:12-13: "They went out, and preached that men should repent. And they cast out many devils, and *anointed with oil* many that were sick, and healed them." This is why I usually carry a bottle of anointing oil with me, as I never know when I will have opportunity to use it. As led by the Holy Spirit, I am prepared to anoint anybody who has the faith and desire to be touched in the name of *Yeshua HaMashiach,* Jesus the Messiah.

Points to Ponder

1. Explain why being a "faith giant" is not a prerequisite for moving in God's power.

2. What is the believer's core purpose in life? How does recognition of this purpose help to set one's priorities right?

3. In your own words, describe the believer's balanced view of Satan and his power.

Notes

1. Biblesoft's New Exhaustive Strong's Numbers and Concordance with Expanded Greek-Hebrew Dictionary, CD-ROM, Biblesoft, Inc. and International Bible Translators, Inc. (1994, 2003, 2006) s.v. "seleniazomai" (NT 4583).

2. *Westminster Shorter Catechism,* http://www.reformed.org/documents/WSC.html (accessed November 2, 2013).

Chapter 8

DEMONSTRATE THE GOSPEL!

"The just shall live by his faith…" (Hab. 2:4). The Septuagint explains that it is "by faith in Me." The Speaker is God. When we live by faith, we walk in divine health day by day. "My righteous one shall live by faith…" (Heb. 10:38 NASB).

In the Hebrew, the key word meaning "faith" is *emunah*. It is translated in the following ways (with the number of occurrences in parentheses): faith (1), faithful (3), faithfully (8), faithfulness (25), honestly (1), responsibility (1), stability (1), steady (1), trust (2), truth (5).

Every shade of meaning is vital but "faithfulness" (loyalty) is the most frequent rendering.

Therefore to live by faith does not mean only to do exploits, but to abide in a continual state of loyalty toward God and His ways. When we live this way, He is our Physician and Healer. According to the dictionary, faithfulness means:

1. [Being] strict or thorough in the performance of a duty: *a faithful worker*

2. [Being] true to one's word, promises, vows, etc.

3. [Being] steady in allegiance or affection; loyal; constant: *faithful friends*

4. [Being] reliable… [How rare is that?]

5. Adhering or true to fact…accurate: *a faithful account*[1]

Be faithful today and always.

To accomplish exploits for the Lord like those we read of in the Bible (and the "greater works" Jesus promised), we need to be obedient—not only to the moral precepts outlined in the Word, but also to the Lord's specific, personal instructions to us. This keeps us well. To obey is better than sacrifice. "For rebellion is as the sin of witchcraft, and stubbornness is as iniquity and idolatry. Because thou hast rejected the word of the LORD, he hath also rejected thee from being king" (1 Samuel 15:22-23).

Somebody has said that we are unfit and unworthy to rule over men if we are not willing that God should rule over us. A helpful prayer along these lines is:

> Lord, as I reconsecrate myself to Your service today, help me not to reject Your specific instructions and thus be eliminated from Your service!

Simple Gospel, Sinful City

For years I have been fascinated with the apostle Paul's missionary journeys. After showing little success in Athens, Paul felt called to the seaport city of Corinth, one of the worldliest and most pagan places in his day.

Paul was a great intellectual, yet he determined with renewed vigor at Corinth to preach with utter simplicity, wholly dependent upon the supernatural power of God. In his letter to the Corinthian believers, here is how Paul expressed his newfound determination:

> For Christ [the Messiah] *did not send me to* [see how many I could] *baptize, but to preach the gospel, not in cleverness of speech, so that the cross of Christ would not be made void. For the word of the cross is foolishness to those who are perishing, but to us who are being saved it is the power of God* (1 Corinthians 1:17-18 NASB).

Paul's heartfelt words to the church of God in Corinth should guide us today. We can argue against evolution and all the trends of our increasingly secular (some would say pagan) society, but we should remember that we have a predecessor: Paul also ministered in a very lost and pagan world. Yet he won believers in Corinth by the simple preaching of the Cross (as he put it). Corinth was mentioned in Homer's *Illiad*. It was a highly strategic, cosmopolitan place to preach the Gospel. Merchants converted in Corinth (the capital of a Roman province) would potentially take the Gospel to the ends of the earth.

The name *Corinth* was synonymous with debauchery; Corinthians took pride in every kind of lust, much like people in the world today. With a temple dedicated to Aphrodite, the city was known for its idolatry and moral corruptions. Paul catalogued these (including deviate sex and fornication) in First Corinthians chapter 6. (The Greek word for "fornication" was *pornea,* from which is derived the English word *pornography.*)

Eighteen verses in Acts chapter 18 narrate and summarize Paul's time in Corinth. He lodged with fellow tent-makers Aquila and Priscilla, and as was his *modus operandi*, he taught Messiah in the synagogue. But when rejected by organized religion, Paul set up shop next door to the synagogue with a convert named Justus. Still, the leader of the synagogue, Crispus, and his family all became believers in Yeshua!

Encouraging the Apostle

Paul came to Corinth dejected and cautious after his near failure in Athens, and after much opposition and the wear and tear of going from city to city. He needed a word of encouragement and guidance. Not until his associates Silas and Timothy arrived from Thessalonica did Paul spring back into his real personality.

Paul was a spiritual giant, yet like all of us, he was a human being whose spirit needed refreshing. Silas and Timothy brought encouraging news about the brethren in Thessalonica staying true to the faith. Up until the time of their arrival, Paul had only visited the synagogue once a week to reason with his fellow Jews. Along with Aquila and Priscilla, he filled his mind and days with tent-making. But the Lord intervened by addressing Paul in a dream and said: "Don't keep silent and don't be afraid to speak" (see Acts 18:9). The Lord assured Paul he would come to no harm and that many Corinthians were predestined for salvation.

What a word! Dreams and visions are a very important part of being a Spirit-led disciple. When we are in the will of God, the Lord will communicate with us, primarily through His Word but also through an audible voice if necessary, as well as through dreams, visions, prophetic words, and so forth.

Reenergenized by hearing directly from the Lord and by the arrival of his coworkers, Paul did not resort to oratory techniques that others used to gain fame and a following. He depended entirely on the Holy Spirit, going from reasoning with the people to testifying.

Reasoning can result in arguments, but testifying to what the Lord has done for us cannot easily be disputed. Testifying is even more powerful than reasonings and disputings. Here's why: I can try to convince people that God wants them to be saved and healed, and they can argue against my doctrine. What they cannot argue with is my experience. How can they refute the fact that I was dying as a child when the Lord appeared to me and gloriously healed me? How can they deny that what the doctors could not do, Dr. Jesus did in one house call!

So Paul did not depend upon the captivating oratory that Greeks greatly admired. He did not count on his great intellect or speaking ability, although he no doubt enjoyed a high IQ. It was the Holy Spirit through Paul who persuaded the Corinthians of a saving knowledge of Messiah. Paul said he was determined to demonstrate the Spirit's power, and not his own. In the end, it is possible to be eloquent without being credible.

Demonstration of the Gospel

The word *demonstration* carries the idea of verification and proof that the Gospel and the resurrection of Jesus are facts. The word *demonstration* indicates a showing off, a show and tell of the Lord's power and presence.

Paul's demonstration of the Gospel with signs, wonders, words of knowledge, wisdom, and healings made him a very credible emissary of the Lord. The proofs undoubtedly were the miracles he performed, along with the gift of tongues, and the conversions of sinners.

Paul demonstrated the Gospel's power because the Holy Spirit imparted through Paul a peace, joy, and happiness the Corinthians had never known. The Gospel had the power to transform their lives from hopeless paganism. Drunkards became sober citizens; thieves turned honest; lust was conquered; profane people learned reverence; lazy souls became purpose-driven; the sick were healed; and mean-spirited troublemakers became peaceful. This is the kind of evidence no one can deny. There was no doubt that Paul's ministry was supernatural. Paul was resolved and determined to preach one message and one message only: Jesus the Messiah crucified to make atonement for sins and sicknesses, and the Cross, the monument of forgiveness.

Yeshua, the Messiah's Hebrew name, was Paul's constant theme. We can learn from his focus on the person of *Yeshua HaMasiach,* Jesus the Messiah and His Lordship. Paul stressed how Jesus fulfilled the ancient prophecies, and how He would come again to rule. These matters are at the heart of the Gospel.

Just as Paul's preaching rejected vain philosophy and extolled only Messiah and Him crucified (with all the benefits of the Cross), the modern-day preacher's job is to display the banner of the Cross, inviting all people to cling to it and take shelter under it.

I wonder how Paul's message compares to today's preaching, with so much emphasis on self-improvement and success. Whatever other knowledge Paul had—and he was greatly educated having sat at the feet of the renowned Rabbi Gamaliel—Messiah's atoning death and its benefits comprised the only knowledge Paul believed both important and urgent to share.

The Great Leveler

Because Messiah's crucifixion was Paul's central message, it challenged the pride and wisdom of the Greeks. One of the results of responding to the Gospel is humility. Thus the Cross is the great leveler—it pulls out the rug from under all human pride. The Lord Himself provided the greatest example of all: He humbled Himself by enduring the lowest death imaginable.

When we are confronted with the message of the Cross, we learn that we are sinners who have absolutely nothing to offer God for our redemption. We cannot earn our salvation; nor can we contribute a single good deed to merit it. We must come God's way, the way of the Cross, trusting in the only Savior and His blood to save us and cleanse us from our sins.

Time has not changed this message. It is just as revolutionary today as it was when Paul preached it. The apostle was "into" the demonstration of the Spirit in a big way, trusting the Lord for signs and wonders to confirm the Gospel, just as Jesus had promised.

In the Great Commission, the Lord said: "These signs will follow those who believe: in My name, they will cast out demons…and if they drink anything deadly, it will by no means hurt them; they will lay hands on the sick and they will recover" (Mark 16:17-18 NKJV). The question is: are we willing to be like Paul—determined and single-minded to demonstrate the Gospel? Paul literally fulfilled the Great Commission's description. He spoke with new tongues; he laid hands on the sick and they recovered; he cast out devils; he cast off snakes; no poison harmed him. When Paul was bitten by a deadly snake on the isle of Malta, he simply shook off the creature and kept going, with no ill effects. This demonstration of Gospel power caused people to marvel and to believe. (See Acts 28:1-5.)

Co-Laborers with God

To demonstrate the Holy Spirit takes faith and practice and learning how to co-labor with God in the Gospel. Men and women who have learned this have a track record of miracles, signs, and wonders.

The result of encounters with the Holy Spirit by great servants of God such as the apostle Paul, the famous nineteenth-century American revivalist Charles Finney, and evangelist Reinhard Bonnke in our own generation are well documented.

When Finney preached, multitudes were saved. Likewise, when Bonnke preaches, multitudes receive the Savior. In Reinhard Bonnke's meetings in Africa and also in our own Gospel festivals, my husband and I witness the demonstration of the Holy Spirit as blind eyes are opened and cripples walk, leap, and run!

In the Book of Acts, Philip the Evangelist had a similar *modus operandi*. Like Paul, Philip preached Christ only. He did not preach success; he was not a "life coach" preacher. Philip preached Messiah. And what were the results? With loud shrieks, demons came out of people, and cripples walked (see Acts 8).

Because God is no respecter of persons, this has been our experience also. When we preach the Gospel in open-air meetings we see demons manifest, the lame walk, people are saved, and (like Philip's campaign in Samaria), great joy erupts among the people.

That is the level of activity the apostle Paul spoke of concerning the "demonstration of the Spirit's power." He meant that the Holy Spirit would authenticate the Gospel with signs and wonders.

Holy Spirit Interruptions

When the Holy Spirit is present, preaching is easy. Sometimes the preacher has to stop preaching; because the demonstration is so powerful, he or she is sidelined! This, of course, is not always the case because God has ordained preaching as His method of winning souls.

For example, when the apostle Peter preached in Cornelius' house in Acts 10:44, the Holy Spirit interrupted the sermon. The Gentiles assembled there experienced their own Pentecost as they began to speak in tongues! What a demonstration of the Spirit's power!

In studying the exploits of Charles Finney, I read about a particular demonstration of the Spirit that occurred in one of his meetings. Many in his audience had never attended a Gospel meeting, and Finney said they looked sullen and angry. When he had been speaking for about a quarter of an hour, an awesome sense of solemnity settled upon the people. Something supernatural "flashed over the congregation—a kind of shimmering" as if the atmosphere had been agitated.[2] Suddenly, the congregation began to fall from their seats, in every direction, crying for mercy.

Finney said, "They fell as fast as lightning. Nearly the entire congregation were on their knees or prostrate." It was a holy chaos. Because of this Holy Spirit shock wave, Finney stopped preaching and joyously shouted, "You are not in hell yet…"[3] And so he directed those souls to the Lord, one by one.

A similar supernatural atmosphere happened while we were holding a revival at a school in Arabia. Like many meetings in the East to this day, the men were seated separately from the women and were required to attend in their role as masters at the school. Most of them looked disinterested and many sat with their arms folded. I began to share from my heart a simple Gospel message from the Book of Matthew, where Jesus said: "Whoever confesses Me before men, him I will also confess before My Father who is in heaven. But whoever denies Me before men, him I will also deny before My Father who is in heaven" (Matt. 10:32-33 NKJV).

Suddenly the Holy Spirit permeated the atmosphere, and both men and women began to shake under His power and to run forward, falling on their knees and confessing the most vile sins and praying to the Lord for forgiveness. Locked-up secrets were exposed, and they were not afraid to confess and to seek forgiveness.

His Power, Not Ours

What causes the Holy Spirit to honor preaching like that? I believe Paul gave us the key when he said that he determined in Corinth to be totally and utterly dependent upon the Lord and not upon himself. He wrote: "For I resolved to know nothing while I was with you except Jesus Christ and him crucified. I came to you in weakness and fear, with much trembling. My message and my preaching were not with wise and persuasive words, but with a demonstration of the Spirit's power, so that your faith might not rest on human wisdom, but on God's power" (1 Cor. 2:2-5 NIV). This is what releases the demonstration of the Spirit. Paul's ministry included prophetic acts, and as an evangelist, he was sometimes dramatic. How shall I describe it? The minister morphs by the power of the Holy Spirit into another person altogether and does and says things that he or she would not normally do.

This type of transformation was seen in the life of Saul, Israel's first king, in First Samuel 10:6. The prophet Samuel told Saul: "The Spirit of the LORD will come upon thee, and thou shalt prophesy with them, and shalt be turned into another man." That is exactly what happened; it was a very dramatic and uncharacteristic scene.

When the apostle Paul was rejected in the Corinthian synagogue, after repeated visits, he (under the inspiration of the Holy Spirit) made a dramatic gesture. He shook off the dust from his clothes, as Jesus had instructed His disciples to do when a city rejected them (see Luke 9:5; 10:11). Quoting from Ezekiel 33, Paul warned, "Your blood be on your own heads!" (NASB).

Those were the words of a faithful watchman. Paul was warning them and us: If you ignore the warnings God gives through His Gospel messengers, you will have no grounds to complain on Judgment Day. Paul shook his clothes and announced that he would take the Gospel instead to the Gentiles, who would receive him.

Of course, we know from studying the life and writings of the apostle Paul that he never rejected the Jewish people. While his prophetic act in Corinth was a true demonstration of the Spirit—and Paul really did go to the Gentiles—this was a warning and not a rejection. Paul testified in his letter to the Romans that he lived with continual heartache, day in and day out, for his fellow Jews to be saved. Like Moses, he was willing to allow his name to be blotted out of the Lamb's Book of Life in order that they might be saved.

Taking Paul's Example

How does Paul's experience in Corinth apply to us? We all need to know that God is with us! When the Lord appeared to Paul in a dream in Corinth, Yeshua the Messiah reassured him with words that we can take to heart as a living word: "Then spake the Lord to Paul in the night by a vision, Be not afraid, but speak, and hold not thy peace: for I am with thee, and no man shall set on thee to hurt thee: for I have much people in this city" (Acts 18:9-10).

That is the kind of assurance we need to hear, isn't it? Just as Yeshua said to Paul, "I am with you," so too, He has promised never to leave nor to forsake His own. Therefore, He is with us whenever and wherever we share the Gospel.

We will not always be immune to danger, just as Paul was not always immune. But with the Lord, we can do all things (see Phil. 4:13). He will give us the strength, wisdom, ability, and demonstration of His Holy Spirit. The Lord also assured Paul that "there are many in this city who are My people" (see Acts 18:10). The people with whom we share the Gospel will always include some whom Yeshua has predestined as His own.

While some hearts are hard ground and unresponsive, there are others who have been waiting all their lives for someone to tell them about Jesus, and to pray for their needs. These hearts are good soil; when we sow the seeds of God's Word and pray for these sick, they receive. When I travel in Asia, it hurts to hear Muslims or Hindus say that nobody ever shared the Gospel with them. Although the Corinthians were totally pagan, God had chosen some of them to become His people.

There are many individuals you can reach who have no understanding of salvation, but have been chosen by God to respond as the Gospel is preached and as you offer to pray for their needs. When this happens, the Gospel is demonstrated!

But will they hear? That's the question Paul asked in Romans 10:14-15:

> *But how are men to call upon him in whom they have not believed? And how are they to believe in him of whom they have never heard? And how are they to hear without a preacher? And how can men preach unless they are sent? As it is written, "How beautiful are the feet of those who preach good news!"* (Romans 10:14-15 RSV).

That is why someone like me and like you must preach Jesus the Messiah and expect the demonstration of the Holy Spirit! "Then the disciples went out and preached everywhere, and the Lord worked with them and confirmed his word by the signs that accompanied it" (Mark 16:20 NIV).

Notice the order! *They* took the initiative and went, and then the Lord worked with them and confirmed their Gospel message with healings and miracles!

Points to Ponder

1. What is the importance of demonstrating the utter simplicity of the Gospel, as Paul did?

2. How did the simplicity of the Gospel impact the people of Corinth? How might this apply today?

3. Why must we be careful not to prejudge or write off those who know nothing of salvation? While not all may respond, does the Bible teach that some will respond?

Notes

1. Faithfulness. Dictionary.com, *Dictionary.com Unabridged,* Random House, Inc., http://dictionary.reference.com/browse/Faithfulness (accessed: October 23, 2013).

2. Charles E. Hambrick-Stowe, *Charles G. Finney and the Spirit of American Evangelism* (Grand Rapids, MI: Wm. B. Eerdmans Publishing Co., 1996), 38.

3. Ibid.

Chapter 9

WHAT IS THE UNFORGIVABLE SIN?

Frequently people write to me seeking some sort of assurance because they are troubled by the unforgivable sin mentioned in the New Testament. Many people cannot receive their healing because Satan has convinced them that they have committed an unpardonable sin. As a result, they live in a state of self-condemnation and doubt. It is a life of defeat and uncertainty, weak in faith, and ignorant of God's Word.

This is a topic that should be discussed in a healing book because many people who are troubled about the unforgivable sin are deprived of healing. Also, those who are uncertain and weak in faith are more susceptible to cynics who ridicule miracles and healings and attribute the wonderful miracles of God to the devil.

Basically, the unforgivable sin is the sin of rejecting God and the Holy Spirit's testimony. Many today worry about blaspheming the Holy Spirit. This is indeed a serious sin; but if you are worried about it, your concern indicates a conscience tender toward God. And so you are certainly not guilty of this sin.

In fact, we should be more concerned about any sin we knowingly commit or stubbornly refuse to abandon because—when you think about it—all sins are "unforgivable" unless we repent!

Isn't that ultimately true? If we die in our sins, and our sins have not been pardoned, then all of our sins would technically be unforgiven.

In order for our sins to be forgiven, covered, blotted out, and atoned for, we must repent now in this lifetime and look by faith to the living blood of Jesus to wash us free from the guilt stains of sin. This is the Good News of the Gospel: that forgiveness of sins has been procured by the passion, the atoning work of Yeshua.

Other sins against the Holy Spirit are mentioned in the Bible— these are forgivable but are nevertheless dangerous. Because of the Holy Spirit's constant activity in this world, it is possible for us to sin against Him by: (notice the progression) resisting the Spirit, quenching the Spirit, grieving the Spirit, insulting the Spirit, and, heaven forbid, by ultimately blaspheming the Spirit. Lest we be guilty of sinning against the Spirit, let us examine these sins against the Spirit mentioned in the Bible.

Resisting the Spirit is spiritually foolish. In Acts 7:51-52, Stephen, the first Christian martyr, rebuked religious people in his generation for resisting the Holy Spirit. He said they had always resisted the Spirit by persecuting the prophets (many of whom predicted Messiah's coming). People today still resist the Holy Spirit every time they refuse to believe Bible testimonies and prophecies or refuse to obey the Gospel and believe in Yeshua as Savior, Deliverer, and Healer. Many professing believers today resist the Spirit by denying the Second Coming and by living carelessly as if the Lord will never return.

When you sense the Holy Spirit trying to get your attention, do not resist Him. Yield to Him! We can train ourselves to yield to the Holy Spirit more and more.

Quenching the Spirit is another sin mentioned in the Bible. To quench means to put out or extinguish";[1] in other words, to stifle or stop. The apostle Paul gave a succinct warning in First Thessalonians 5:19: "Quench not the Spirit." I like the God's Word version's rendering: "Don't put out the Spirit's fire."

We can also *grieve the Holy Spirit.* Paul's warning is recorded in Ephesians 4:30: "And do not grieve the Holy Spirit of God, by whom you were sealed for the day of redemption" (NKJV).

King David begged God not to take His Spirit from him (see Ps. 51:11). Since the Holy Spirit dwells within our mortal bodies and we are the temple of God, the Holy Spirit shrinks and shies away from ill conduct and corrupt speech. It is often observed that He is a gentleman who distances Himself when insulted or the atmosphere is displeasing.

If you are sensitive to the Holy Spirit, you can sense when His presence lifts like a gentle dove flying away. This often happens when believers become carelessly profane, unruly, or ribald.

There are degrees of sinning against the Spirit, and even more dangerous is *insulting the Spirit of God*. The writer of Hebrews warned that we can do "despite unto the Spirit of grace." (Heb. 10:29) The Revised Standard Version describes the Spirit of grace being outraged. The context pertains to willful sin and conduct that disregards the precious blood of the Messiah, considering it as a common thing, and resulting in a fearful and fiery judgment from God. This is a warning that people who profess to be believers can become deceived and hardened by sin to the point that they insult the Spirit through outrageous conduct and slander. Yeshua's words and works were a clear evidence of the ministry of the Holy Spirit working in and through Him as the Anointed One, the Messiah of the Bible. But a heart can become so hard against Yeshua that repentance is not possible.

What Is Blasphemy against the Holy Spirit?

Blasphemy against the Holy Spirit is the sin of ascribing the work of the Holy Spirit to Satan. It is attributing the power of Yeshua to an unclean spirit. This happened in Mark 3 and Matthew 12. Jesus said all blasphemies will be forgiven, even blasphemies against Him; but why did He say blasphemy against the Holy Spirit is unforgivable?

This is the reason: When someone concludes that Yeshua's power is demonic, that person has clearly rejected the evidence which produces saving faith in Him. Therefore the blasphemer has rejected the efforts of God to save him from his sins through the Atonement of Yeshua. When somebody is hardened in this way and willing to believe that Yeshua was in league with the devil, saving faith in the Savior is not possible!

But suppose you have been tempted with dark thoughts against the Holy Spirit. Perhaps the devil has wanted to torment you and cause you to lose the assurance of your salvation by tempting you with blasphemous thoughts against the Holy Spirit. I want to assure you that having dark thoughts and struggles in your mind does not mean you have sinned the unpardonable sin.

Satan will attempt to deceive you in this area: he will try to torment you, because demons are malignant and vicious. But do not believe his lies for a second. No one who genuinely loves God, believes in the Gospel, and clings to the Messiah by faith, has sinned the unforgivable sin—even if Satan has tempted that person with dark, tormenting thoughts.

Always have the presence of mind to speak to the mountain and to rebuke demonic thoughts in the name of Yeshua. Satan can suggest all sorts of thoughts to your mind. But what does the Bible say? "Submit yourself therefore to God, resist Satan, and he *will* flee from you" (see James 4:7).

In conclusion, how can committing the unforgivable sin be prevented? We must walk carefully in the power of the Holy Spirit, making sure that we are not guilty of grieving, quenching, or insulting Him, and sliding down the slippery slope that leads to blasphemy.

We must be careful not to reject the testimony of the Spirit, for He is the one who testifies of Yeshua. If we reject the Holy Spirit, we can reject and neglect the Lord's "great salvation."

Loved by the Holy Spirit

Do not be afraid of the Holy Spirit. He is so very precious. He is described in the New Testament as the Comforter, the Person of the Godhead who stays with us 24/7 and guides us into all truth. Many people fear they have crossed the line and somehow committed the unpardonable sin, but if you love God, that is a lie from the pit of hell!

The Holy Spirit cares for us and loves us dearly. We are precious to Him; there are many scriptures to assure us that He is working for good in our lives and guiding us into all truth.

Pray with me now a prayer of assurance:

Heavenly Father, I do believe in my heart that You raised Yeshua from the dead, and He is Lord. Forgive me of all of my sins and forgive me for times when I may have resisted the Holy Spirit. Come, Holy Spirit, regenerate me into newness of life that I may serve the Lord and help to bring His kingdom! Thank You, Lord, that healing and peace of mind are mine, in Jesus' name, amen and amen!

Points to Ponder

1. Are you worried about whether or not you have blasphemed the Holy Spirit? What does your worried state tell you?

2. How do we sin against the Holy Spirit in our everyday lives? How should we respond when we become aware that we have sinned against Him?

3. What is the ultimate loss resulting from the rejection of the Holy Spirit?

Note

1. Quench. Dictionary.com, Dictionary.com Unabridged, Random House, Inc., http://dictionary.reference.com/browse/quench (accessed: November 04, 2013).

Chapter 10

Divine Health: Habits
of Spiritual People

What are some of the habits of truly spiritual people who are healthy both mentally and physically?

The Prayer Habit

Of course, prayer is habit number one. James 5:16 says that "the effectual fervent prayer of a righteous man availeth much."

The Old Testament prophet Daniel had the habit of praying three times a day at his window, which faced in the direction of Jerusalem and God's holy Temple Mount. It is interesting that Jewish Law makes it a duty to pray three times a day (morning prayer, afternoon prayer, and prayer at nightfall), but the apostle Paul exhorted us in First Thessalonians 5:17: "Pray without ceasing."

In the morning, truly spiritual people offer the day to the Lord before going about their routines. Then, before retiring at night, they examine their consciences before falling to sleep; they want to be sure that the sun is not going down on their anger or upon any unconfessed sin before retiring. This releases a person night and day to have the peace of God that passes all understanding, without the stress of strife and the tension of a guilty conscience.

The Praise and Giving Habits

Truly one of the greatest secrets of spiritual people is their attitude of praise. They have learned how to be thankful and to offer up praise to the Lord. King David praised Him seven times a day (see Ps. 119:164). Praise releases joy, which in turn brings strength (see Neh. 8:10).

Spiritual people are also givers. Not only do they give the first fruits of their increase to the Lord their Maker, but they constantly give to others. Proverbs 11:24 observes that "There is one who scatters, yet increases more; and there is one who withholds more than is right, but it leads to poverty" (NKJV).

I would rather be generous than stingy, wouldn't you? There is a joy that comes with cheerful giving that is healthy.

The Fasting Habit

Truly spiritual people also make a regular habit of adding fasting to their prayers. Some answers are received from God by praying, but some only come after adding fasting to our prayers. When the disciples asked the Lord why their prayers for the "lunatic" boy went unanswered, He said, "this kind does not come out except by prayer and fasting" (see Matt. 17:21).

In our ministry we have the Every Friday Fast, in which we forfeit breakfast or lunch, or some part of our food or drink. We do this during the day on Fridays, while radicals and terrorists are plotting to do evil. This level of corporate fasting restrains and frustrates the powers of darkness in a world that is already spinning out of control.

Things might be a lot worse if spiritual people were not crying out to the Lord day and night with prayers and fastings!

The Word and Faith Habits

A truly spiritual believer reads the Word of God every day. A daily reading plan is ideal, so that the Bible is read through every year.

Healing comes as we read the Bible, because it is a supernatural book that actually "reads" us. The Scriptures bring correction and understanding that lead to healing and deliverance.

Furthermore, a truly spiritual person keeps his or her faith alive. A great danger of our day is to be faith-deficient: Jesus asked a very important question in Luke 18:8: "When the Son of Man comes, will He find faith on the earth?" (NASB).

Frequently I meditate on His words to Peter in Luke 22:32: "I have prayed for you, that your faith may not fail..." (NASB). It is absolutely vital to keep our faith topped up in order to serve family and friends who might desperately need, at any given moment, the prevailing prayer of faith—and not the prayer of unbelief! Do not let your faith become weakened so that it fails in a crisis.

Spiritual people press into God to obtain "like precious faith," the kind of faith mentioned in Second Peter 1:1: "Simon Peter, a servant and an apostle of Jesus Christ, to them that have obtained like precious faith with us through the righteousness of God and our Saviour Jesus Christ...."

Faith Is "Precious"

The Scriptures describe certain things as being precious. We will discuss five in particular: the redemption of the soul, the blood of Christ, Messiah Himself (to His ransomed people), the great promises of the Gospel, and apostolic faith.

In Second Peter 1:1, we learn that faith is precious, or valuable. *God's Word Translation* mentions "a faith that is as valuable as ours." The Holman Christian Standard Bible renders this verse: "To those who have obtained a faith of equal privilege with ours through the righteousness of our God and Savior Jesus Christ."

Have you obtained this "like precious faith"?

True faith is exceedingly precious and costly, as a jewel of great price. It is rare, indeed. Precious faith is the means to obtain a part in the great work of redemption. The word *obtained* in Second Peter 1:1 means "cast lots."[1] The same Greek word is translated *lot* in Luke 1:9

and *obtained* in Acts 1:17. It literally means, "by divine allotment." This implies that faith is a divinely elected gift of God.

The word rendered "like precious" (meaning, equally precious) is found only here in the New Testament. This apostolic faith is precious, but is maintained through the fight of faith, or constant spiritual warfare.

Essentially faith is trust in the promise and character of a Person. Do not despair if you think your faith is not as strong as the apostle Peter's. Because of Jesus' teaching about faith as the grain of mustard seed, your faith *is* "like precious faith" having the power to sustain and heal. This is true whether your faith flame is large or just a spark!

The Spirit of Faith

The spirit of faith described by the apostle Peter is universally resident in all truly spiritual believers. In a similar fashion, Paul said, "We having the same spirit of faith, according as it is written, I believed, and therefore have I spoken; we also believe…" (2 Cor. 4:13). The truly spiritual person therefore will speak faith continually.

Believing speech is repeated with conviction from the pages of the Word of God. It is the kind of speech that speaks to mountains. It is more powerful than any other kind of speech because it has within it the living presence of the Author. "The word of God is living and active…" (Heb. 4:12 NASB).

People can hear the difference between the voice of conviction and the babble of a professional talker. Spiritual people habitually testify to what the Lord has done for them. They have learned that He has committed Himself to confirm the voice of the living Gospel with signs and wonders.

"I believed, and therefore have I spoken…" (2 Cor. 4:13). We today also believe, and therefore we speak God's words with conviction. Where there is true faith, and the true spirit of faith, there will inevitably be an expression of the Lord's healing power, for as "with the heart man believeth unto righteousness, [so] with the mouth confession is made unto salvation [saving health]" (Rom. 10:10).

More Habits of Spiritual People

Another important habit of truly spiritual people—and one to emulate—is that they always declare the faithfulness of God. With their mouths and with their words they magnify the Lord's works and wonders. Rather than cave in to discouragement and despair, they continually and consciously make an effort to extol God's unfailing love and unbreakable promises, under all conditions!

This is the spirit of the overcomer. An overcomer does not easily cave in to sickness and certainly does not run off to the doctor in fear, without first consulting the Holy Spirit.

It can be dangerous to ask people, "How are you?" Some of them give an "organ recital" by running through a whole catalogue of aches or pains. Or they share their heartaches, but ask me to keep praying for them in general.

Nobody can promise that they will keep praying for another person (especially non-family members) *ad infinitum.* To promise or agree out of a spirit of politeness that you will pray into the future for casual acquaintances is dishonest.

Therefore, a habit of spiritual people is to pray for others immediately, on the spot. Since you cannot promise somebody to pray for them indefinitely, it is best to make a habit of praying at the time of the request (as led by the Spirit), concerning whatever situation is troubling them.

For example, a young Muslim man in Jerusalem told me he was suffering from kidney stones. So I prayed for him that very moment. He was shocked that the pain left him instantly.

But why shouldn't the pain leave? Jesus promised in Acts 1:8:

> *But you will receive power when the Holy Spirit has come upon you, and you will be my witnesses in Jerusalem and in all Judea and Samaria, and to the end of the earth* (ESV).

At another time, I prayed for the same young man's car keys to be found when he told me it would cost a considerable amount to buy a new set. "Prayer will find the keys," I said.

After a week, I asked him if the keys had been found, but he just laughed. He never really believed in the first place that his keys would be found, even though Jesus had healed him miraculously from kidney stones. So he was totally shocked when somebody knocked on his door with his car keys. More than a week had gone by since I had prayed, but the keys were found in the middle of a road!

It pays to pray and to dare to speak words of faith!

Truly spiritual people are encouragers. Their words are a tonic to the downhearted. They are not selfish; they give genuine compliments and Spirit-inspired encouragements frequently. They also accept compliments without false modesty, but always speak with humility in general and with graciousness. (This trait has become a rare commodity.) Their words of encouragement are healing; as Scripture testifies: "Pleasant words are as an honeycomb, sweet to the soul, and health to the bones" (Prov. 16:24). And truly spiritual people learn to speak to the mountains in their lives rather than co-existing with them.

Points to Ponder

1. What do you believe Paul meant when he exhorted us to "pray without ceasing"?

2. What is your personal experience with *believing speech?* Is God urging you to grow in this area? How so?

3. Have you ever given an "organ recital"? What did it reveal about your mindset?

Note

1. Biblesoft's New Exhaustive Strong's Numbers and Concordance with Expanded Greek-Hebrew Dictionary, CD-ROM, Biblesoft, Inc. and International Bible Translators, Inc. (1994, 2003, 2006) s.v. "lagchano," (NT 2975).

Chapter 11

HEALING AND THE LAW
OF FIRST MENTION

Healing is not a Gospel accessory that we can pop on or off based on who is listening. In some churches divine healing is never taught. But healing is an integral part of the Gospel! Jesus Himself led the healing charge to vanquish sickness and disease!

I want to reinforce the healing message in our minds, spirits, and bodies from the Gospel of John. It is important that we have firmly established in our hearts that healing is an essential part of the Gospel. We are going to need the healing message in days to come. Hospitals are overcrowded and sometimes riddled with superbugs. Crises and tribulations are on the way that will call for having our own faith. We must prepare now to be strong in this. Earnestly contending for all of the faith once delivered to the saints (see Jude 1:3) is a major call upon my life to prepare the Body of Messiah in light of the fact that overburdened health services might even collapse. Just as the Lord sent many teachers to instruct His Body to get out of debt, He presses upon my spirit continually the need to teach that God is able to keep our spirits, souls, and bodies in troublesome times.

John's Gospel is key. It first of all establishes Yeshua as the Word of God and the Lamb of God who takes away the sin of the world (see John 1:1,29). In John chapter 2, we see the Lord's first miracle, the turning of water into wine. And in chapter 3 we read one of the most important verses in the entire Bible, the Golden Text, John 3:16: "For God so loved the world, that he gave his only begotten Son, that whosoever believeth in him should not perish, but have everlasting life." Jesus spoke these words to Rabbi Nicodemus, who visited Jesus by night and admitted that no human being could have performed the miracles that Jesus did unless God were with Him. The miracles caused Nicodemus to conclude that Yeshua was a teacher from God. Jesus, in turn, perceived that Nicodemus was seeking truth; so He revealed His mission to the rabbi.

Healing in John's Gospel

The Gospel of John references numerous healing miracles. In fact, Jesus performed hundreds, even thousands of healings; the Gospels tell us that He healed multitudes. However, the number of cases specifically recorded is small. Why? Undoubtedly, the healings documented by the Holy Spirit are for specific teaching purposes.

In John chapter 4, Jesus revisited Cana, where He had transformed six jars of water into wine. There, His healing power was urgently sought by a certain nobleman whose son lay sick and dying about twenty-three miles away, in Capernaum. The nobleman had perhaps heard about the water-into-wine miracle at Cana, or some other miracle of healing. But why is the particular healing of his son (who was cured by Jesus from a distance), the first healing recorded in John's Gospel?

There is a principle that Bible scholars refer to as the "law of the first mention." This spiritual law teaches us to study the passages in which a doctrine is mentioned for the first time in order to extract the fundamental, inherent elements of the doctrine. So we will read the account in John chapter 4 to uncover some fundamentals about divine healing:

Once more he visited Cana in Galilee, where he had turned the water into wine. And there was a certain royal official whose son lay sick at Capernaum. When this man heard that Jesus had arrived in Galilee from Judea, he went to him and begged him to come and heal his son, who was close to death. "Unless you people see miraculous signs and wonders," Jesus told him, "you will never believe."
The royal official said, "Sir, come down before my child dies." Jesus replied, "You may go. Your son will live." The man took Jesus at his word and departed. While he was still on the way, his servants met

him with the news that his boy was living. When he inquired as to the
time when his son got better, they said to him, "The fever left him
yesterday at the seventh hour."
Then the father realized that this was the exact time at which Jesus
had said to him, "Your son will live." So he and all his household be-
lieved (John 4:46–53 NIV).

Why didn't Jesus perform great miracles in His hometown of
Nazareth, just a few miles from Cana? The Gospels do not state that He
would not do any mighty works in Nazareth, but that he *could* not perform miracles there because of the Nazarenes' unbelief (see Matt. 13:58).
First of all, it is interesting that Yeshua limited Himself to the same conditions that any of us routinely meet in ministering to the sick. Although
He was God, Jesus did not override the will of the people.

Years ago we were divinely led to Nazareth to hold Gospel meetings outdoors on a hill next door to a mosque. The Lord wonderfully
met us there, and some significant healings took place. Even my trans-
lator was healed.

We had advertised the meetings this way: "Jesus of Nazareth Finds a
Generation of Faith." Being a generation of faith is critical. Jesus will always heal—even in His hometown of Nazareth—*if He finds faith!*

Principles from John 4

The miracle healing of the boy in John 4 teaches some very specific
principles that will help us both to be healed and to minister healing to
others. Let us search them out:

Petition the Lord Directly

The first principle we learn about the healing of the nobleman's son
in John 4 is that we must come to the Lord and petition Him directly!
Yeshua is the Great Physician. Healing is His to impart, and it is free—
absolutely no charge. We do not know whether this nobleman had
consulted with other physicians, because the Bible does not tell us. We
do know that his son was dying. We also know that as a court official,

he had the financial means and access to physicians to pay for a cure, if one was available.

But any possible remedy had already resulted in failure. Perhaps Jesus was the man's last resort. People tend to put their trust in doctors first, and so their faith in God can be divided, diluted, or nonexistent. Many times in Gospel meetings in Third World countries we see people place themselves totally in God's hands. These impoverished souls have no medical resources; therefore, He is their only hope. With no choice but to believe God, they are healed, in His love and mercy!

We have seen the same wonderful results in our Gospel meetings in Africa and Asia where God has healed poor folks with no financial means to visit hospitals and doctors.

Our End Is His Beginning

The second principle to note about divine healing in this account is that God's miracles begin where man's abilities end. The nobleman's son was at the point of death, so all other means of a cure were now exhausted. There was no hope outside of a miracle. Either God would intervene, or the boy would die.

When all other possibilities are finished, God's healing power can be made manifest, to His glory! This should be a great encouragement. There is no impossible case when God is petitioned.

Our Desperation Leads Us to Him

A third principle about divine healing is the father's desperation, which forced him to take faith actions. His request was very simple, just as the Bible teaches: "Ask and you shall receive!"

Jesus said in John 16:24: "Hitherto have ye asked nothing in my name: ask, and ye shall receive, that your joy may be full." James 5:16 declares "the effectual fervent prayer of a righteous man avails much!"

Let us examine Jesus' *modus operandi,* which should also be ours. He handled each case individually through the gifts of the Spirit: the discerning of spirits, the word of knowledge, and so forth.

Jesus perceived that this nobleman craved a miraculous sign. He said: "Unless you see signs and wonders you will not believe." What do we learn from the Lord's rebuke? We should learn not to fall into the trap of demanding a sign from Him! It is always a temptation to ask the Lord for advance proof. However, the Lord's desire is that we *only believe* (see Mark 5:36). To *only believe* is to trust in Him only! As an old hymn goes: "Only believe, only believe. All things are possible, only believe."

Humility Is Required

Do not expect special treatment. Perhaps this nobleman was a member of King Herod's court, as is the conjecture of some Bible scholars. Because of his position he may have expected VIP treatment.

Prominent people are accustomed to being served and fawned over. For example, in the Old Testament, the Syrian general Naaman contracted the dreaded disease of leprosy (see 2 Kings 5). He was informed that there was a prophet in Israel who could heal him, so he left Syria to find Elisha.

General Naaman presumed that his rank and prominence would cause the prophet to stand on ceremony. Instead, Elisha sent a short message advising Naaman to dip himself seven times in the Jordan River, and he would be healed!

Naaman balked. He had expected Elisha to meet with him, call on the name of the Lord, or wave his hand over the sickness. Instead, the prophet seemed to treat him impersonally, via a message. Namaan felt snubbed; he certainly did not believe that the Jordan River had supernatural power. However, by the grace of God, he took the advice and humbled himself. In the end, he followed Elisha's instructions and did not allow pride to rob his chance to be healed! He dipped seven times in the Jordan, and was so grateful to be healed that he offered rewards to the prophet. Know this: you cannot buy healing. All who minister healing should also take note: the Bible makes it very clear we should never be motivated in ministry by a person's rank, wealth, or position.

Do Not Be Moved by Rank, Money, or Power

Notice the noble stance of our Lord. When responding to a person of high rank, there was no obsequious fawning. Nor did Yeshua reject the man on the basis of his class.

Yeshua also dared to test the nobleman with an open rebuke: "Unless you see signs and wonders you won't believe."

Thankfully, the nobleman was indeed noble and benefited from the rebuke! Many persons (like General Naaman) too easily take offense. In this case, the nobleman was required to demonstrate simple trusting faith in the Lord's word without being given any other sign!

Jesus was saying, "You must become active in this healing. Let Me see your faith. Do not expect Me to bear all the responsibility." Ever the Teacher with an eye on our long-term benefit, Jesus often told those who sought His help: "Let it be according to *your* faith."

Distance Is Not a Problem

The nobleman said to Yeshua, "Sir, my son is going to die unless You come."

Capernaum was quite a distance away. Yeshua experienced the same dilemmas that we face today. You and I could jump in a car or take a taxi from Cana to Capernaum to pray for somebody. But should we take the time to travel the distance and pray for the need? Or should we pray by proxy?

In each case we should be led by the Holy Spirit. Sometimes Jesus went to the home to minister; but in this case, He apparently perceived that reaching the distance involved would be too time-consuming. Or, perhaps He wanted the distressed father to learn to take Him at His word.

In any case, the Lord decided to speak the word of healing. "Go thy way," He said boldly, "your son lives." Hallelu-Yah! The man believed the word of the Lord and, as he departed, did not complain or express any doubts.

That was commendable faith! The Jamieson, Fausset and Brown Commentary states that "The man believed the word, and the cure shooting quicker than lightning from Cana to Capernaum, was felt by the dying youth."[1]

It is wonderful that Jesus taught us by example to cast out demons and to pray for the sick through the laying on of hands or the anointing with oil. But in John 4 He showed that someone can be healed from a distance, when we speak the word of deliverance.

Today, we might do that on the telephone, in a letter, or via the Internet.

Scripture says: "He sent forth his word, and healed them, and delivered them from destruction" (Ps. 107:20 RSV). That is healing from a distance. The Bible provides two other great "healing by distance" examples:

In Matthew 8:8, a centurion petitioned Jesus: "Sir, I don't deserve to have you come into my house. But just give a command, and my servant will be healed" (GW). "Jesus told the officer, 'Go! What you believed will be done for you.' And at that moment the servant was healed" (Matt. 8:13 GW).

In Matthew 15, a Canaanite woman revealed her faith:

> *...A Canaanite woman from that region came out and was crying, "Have mercy on me, O Lord, Son of David; my daughter is severely oppressed by a demon."...And he answered, "It is not right to take the children's bread and throw it to the dogs." She said, "Yes, Lord, yet even the dogs eat the crumbs that fall from their masters' table." Then Jesus answered her, "O woman, great is your faith! Be it done for you as you desire." And her daughter was healed instantly* (Matthew 15:22, 26-28 ESV).

The Spoken Word Is Powerful

So we see the principle that there is power in the spoken word. Jesus' first recorded healing in the Gospel of John was not accomplished by the laying on of hands, nor by some other tangible means such as anointing with oil or prayer cloths. It was accomplished by what I call first-class faith: by *speaking* the word of healing, and by speaking to the mountain!

May we learn that taking the Lord at His Word and speaking to the mountain is the most direct way to be healed! Thank God, we already have His Word recorded in the Bible with many precious healing promises! (See Exodus 15:26; Psalms 103:1-5; Proverbs 4:20-23; Isaiah 53:4-5; Matthew 8:16-17; Mark 1:40-44; Mark 16:17-18; Luke 4:17-19; Acts 10:38; Galatians 3:13; First Peter 2:24; James 5:13-16; Third John 2.)

The Word Tries Us

Psalms 105:19 says, "the word of the Lord tried him." Have you ever been involved in a trial by the Word of God? Trials are God's way to produce a proven company of saints. Because of my own faith trials with the Lord, Psalms 105:19 is one of my favorite (and most comforting) verses. The subject was Joseph, who was tested by the Lord's many words and promises to him. Joseph believed and came out on top in the end.

It is important that we are tried by God's Word to see of what we are made. God might easily have taken every one of us home to heaven the moment we experienced a saving knowledge of the Lord. There are indeed some babies in heaven who wear crowns, although they have never carried a cross in this world.

But the majority of believers come to eternal bliss out of life's great tribulations and have washed their robes white in the blood of the Lamb.

The nobleman in John chapter 4 was tested, too. Verse 50 records that he believed what Jesus said. Jesus' words surely tried him; he had to return home, seemingly with nothing to show except the words Yeshua spoke into the air.

The *King James Bible* says it was the seventh hour (about 1 P.M.) when Jesus spoke the authoritative word of healing. The man immediately set off on the journey to Capernaum, where his son lay sick. In Bible times, it would be a day's journey home. Imagine how Jesus' words tried him along the way! There was no possibility of the instant gratification and confirmation provided by phones, emails, or text messaging. The father had to keep believing and trusting. No doubt, as he traveled, his heart was less heavy than before, because he had something to which he could cling: the bold healing promise Jesus made. Perhaps he had to spend the night on the road, but the next day he saw his servants approaching with news. Did they look downcast and heavy of heart? No! Their faces were joyful! They had good news. (The Gospel is always good news!) They said, "Your son lives!"

The fever had broken at the same hour that the Lord had spoken the word of life. As a result, the nobleman and his entire household became believers in Yeshua!

Healing is a Process

Healing is a recovery process. Always believe that from the moment you are prayed for (by faith) in the name of Jesus, your healing recovery has begun! It is noteworthy that the healing of the nobleman's son was not instantaneous. At a certain point the fever broke and the young man began to improve.

It was nevertheless a steady recovery. Do not always expect an instant answer; you can, however, expect a full recovery. The account says the boy began to recover from the time the Lord had spoken his healing.

This should encourage believers who are just beginning to step out as instruments of healing. Perhaps you are reluctant to pray for others because you cannot believe for instant results. Take heart: in most cases, divine healing is gradual and not instantaneous.

Think of how patient people are with the medical world. They generously grant doctors, clinics, and hospitals the benefit of time as they wait patiently for the cure. Yet when it comes to the Great Physician, they whine and fall into doubt and unbelief when results are not instantaneous.

What a shame! What duplicity!

Always believe that God honors your faith, all the time. Mark 16:18 declares that one of the signs that will follow and authenticate disciples of the Lord is that we will pray for the sick and they *shall* recover! And remember: recovery implies a steady process.

God's Ways Are Higher

Our ways are not God's ways (see Isa. 55:9). John chapter 4 teaches us that when we make our requests to the Lord, He answers in His way, not ours. He might indeed grant our main desire, but not always in the manner we suppose or imagine.

Initially, in John chapter 4, the nobleman imagined that his son would be healed by Jesus making a visit to Capernaum. Jesus did heal the boy, but not in the exact manner the father had requested. God will graciously hear our prayers and grant our requests, but He always knows the best way to do things. He is not limited to time and space. By the power of His Holy Spirit, He is omnipresent and able to do things we barely dream possible.

Jesus' decision to heal the young man through the spoken word put Psalms 107:20 into action. It is one of my favorite verses: "He sent his word, and healed them, and delivered them from their destructions."

The Word of the Lord has great efficacy and power. Because Jesus is the Creator Incarnate, He addresses our healing in the same way that God spoke worlds into being. When Jesus decrees that we are healed, we are healed!

Faith Rising to the Occasion

The nobleman's faith rose to the occasion. He was willing to believe the word of the Lord and to go on his way without complaining.

Let's review some of the things we have discovered about divine healing, according to the "law of the first mention":

- We have observed that seeking signs and wonders is a trap. The Lord requires simple faith in His spoken, revealed Word.

- We have discovered that the Lord is no respecter of persons: although He came to preach the Gospel to the poor, He was not averse to healing a rich man's son. It was not necessary for Jesus to luxuriate at the nobleman's quarters. Nor did He seek financial reward.

- We have also learned the blessed lesson that there is no distance in God.

- We have learned in the law of first mention concerning healing in John's Gospel that speaking to the mountain (sickness) can be just as effective as the laying on of hands.

Points to Ponder

1. What is the significance of the law of first mention? How does this law affect your approach to Bible study?

2. What can happen when our means are exhausted and we turn to God in desperation? How is faith important in such instances?

3. Describe an experience of being tried by God's Word. How did you feel about it at the time? How do you see the experience now?

Note

1. Jamieson, Fausset and Brown Commentary Electronic Database (Biblesoft, Inc. 2006), s.v. John 4:50.

Chapter 12

HEALING ON THE SABBATH

Remember the Sabbath day, to keep it holy. Six days you shall labor and do all your work, but the seventh day is the Sabbath of the LORD your God. In it you shall do no work [servile labor]*...”* (Exodus 20:8-10 NKJV).

The time, energy, and money accumulated by breaking the fourth commandment may ultimately be forfeited on doctor and hospital bills!

We do not wish to impose on the Church the seventh day or Sunday as a day of rest. Let each believer be convinced in his or her own mind concerning days. As the apostle Paul taught in Romans 14:5: "One person esteems one day above another; another esteems every day alike. Let each be fully convinced in his own mind" (NKJV).

However, I believe we can all agree that a weekly Sabbath rest is necessary for divine health.

The Jewish Sabbath begins at sundown Friday evening and ends twenty-four hours later, on Saturday evening. The *Erev Shabbat* (Friday evening) meal with Sabbath candle lighting is a weekly Jewish holy day of blessings, family feasting, singing, and relaxation. When our family first lived in Israel in the 1980s, we adopted the daily rhythm of the Jewish state, and even now, we still welcome the Shabbat as a time to unwind by late Friday afternoon.

Sabbath-keeping among Evangelicals has become a prophetic phenomenon, a grassroots movement in traditional denominations, as well as among believers who also attend messianic fellowships. A prominent

Pentecostal leader whispered to me, "Don't tell anybody, but our organization now keeps the Sabbath!"

The Holy Spirit has been simultaneously leading many believers worldwide to enjoy the Jewish Sabbath. Don't misunderstand me—you can still worship on Sunday and every day of the week. But please don't call Sunday the Sabbath, because Sunday is not the seventh day. Sunday is *Yom Rishon,* in Hebrew—the first day of the week.

God's Word on the Sabbath

When I was a child I was puzzled by the fact that all of the Ten Commandments were taken at face value in Christianity—except the fourth. The Sabbath was changed by men to Sunday, but my young conscience could not understand why God would change His mind. I am not going to delve further into this still controversial subject. However, it is worth noticing that in many quarters of the Church the Sabbath is being rediscovered.

The Early Church kept the seventh day as the Sabbath and assembled together on *motzei shabbat* (Saturday night) to break bread together because Saturday night was, in Hebraic culture, the official beginning of the first day of the week, the day that Yeshua was raised from the dead.

With many scholars believing that we are already in (or approaching) the seventh sabbatical millennium, the emphasis upon God's sabbaths is present-day truth. The Bible tells us that a thousand years is as a day to the Lord. Many believe we are living in the days of Hosea 6:2, which says: "After two days will he revive us: in the third day, he will raise us up, and we shall live in his sight."

A parallel verse is the riddle Jesus sent to Herod in Luke 13:32: "Go and tell that fox, 'Behold, I cast out demons, and perform cures today and tomorrow and the third day I finish my course'" (ESV).

Isaiah 58:10-11 connects the pouring out of the soul for the hungry and afflicted with having healthy, strong bones (in Hebrew literally "armed"[1] or "armored" bones). This great chapter, Isaiah 58, culminates with a promise that we shall be fed with the heritage of Jacob and ride upon the high places of the earth if we call the Lord's Sabbath a delight and honor the Sabbath by not speaking idle words or seeking our own pleasure (see verses 13-14).

Shall we enter into the blessings of these glorious promises attached to the Sabbath? Has God's Word been broken or changed? I don't think so. Yehovah testifies of Himself, "I am the LORD, I change not..." (Mal. 3:6).

Jesus and the Sabbath

However, we are mainly considering in this chapter, not the correct day of the sabbath, but rather the Lord's mercy of timely healing, *especially* on the Sabbath. The Lord Jesus never broke or desecrated the Sabbath, but He resisted and overruled the religious leaders' foibles and the "traditions of men." The Jewish nation into which the Lord was born held to many regulations that were not prescribed in the Law of Moses. As a result, Jesus received more criticism about His behavior on the Sabbath than any other matter. What He and His disciples did or did not do on the Sabbath became points of contention, with acts of healing eliciting the most attacks from His enemies.

Jesus was a Sabbath observer and never advocated breaking it. He was always to be found in synagogue on the Sabbath, for worship and the public reading of Scripture. In the New Testament, we see Him in faithful attendance in Nazareth on the Sabbath day. In His inaugural address in His home synagogue, He found in the Isaiah scroll a passage about Himself. It defined how He would spend His Sabbaths: "The Spirit of the Lord is upon me, because he hath anointed me to preach the gospel to the poor; he hath sent me to heal the brokenhearted, to preach deliverance to the captives, and recovering of sight to the blind, to set at liberty them that are bruised. To preach the acceptable year of the Lord" (Luke 4:18-19).

In His commentary following the reading of the passage, the Lord's ironic humor is noticeable: "You will undoubtedly say, Physician heal thyself" (see Luke 4:23). Jesus was essentially saying, "You will no doubt expect that after My exploits in Capernaum, I must 'heal' My own town."

Furthermore, Yeshua upbraided His fellows for their lack of faith and insular mindset. He did this by reminding them that in Elijah's day it was a Gentile widow who merited a miracle. He added that in Elisha's day, it was a Gentile Syrian, the leper Naaman, who was granted a miraculous healing.

How thoroughly familiar Jesus was with the Scriptures! For rebuking of the people of Nazareth, He was thrust out in an uproar. In Luke 4:31, we see Him back in Capernaum, faithfully teaching in the synagogues of Galilee on "the sabbath days."

The Sabbath for All

In Luke 4, the first person Yeshua healed (or delivered) was in Capernaum on the Sabbath—a man with an unclean spirit:

> In the synagogue there was a man possessed by the spirit of an unclean demon, and he cried out with a loud voice. "Let us alone! What business do we have with each other, Jesus of Nazareth? Have You come to destroy us? I know who You are—the Holy One of God!" But Jesus rebuked him, saying, "Be quiet and come out of him!" And when the demon had thrown him down in the midst of the people, he came out of him without doing him any harm. And amazement came upon them all, and they began talking with one another, saying, "What is this message? For with authority and power He commands the unclean spirits, and they come out." And the report about Him was spreading into every locality in the surrounding district (Luke 4:33-37 NASB).

Concerning the sanctity of Sabbath observance, the Pharisees in their zeal had instituted many additional rules and prohibitions as a fence or wall to protect the Mosaic Law.

Observant Jews kept the Sabbath from sundown Friday to sundown Saturday. It was a good and righteous thing to do. But the Pharisees and scribes began to define work in some over-the-top and burdensome ways. Thus Jesus made an amazing statement in Mark 2:27: "The Sabbath was made for man, and not [the reverse] man for the Sabbath."

Chew on that wonderful statement for a moment: Jesus broadened the Sabbath's influence, so that it was not just for the Hebrews, but for all mankind. In effect, He taught that the Sabbath was intended to be a universal blessing, a day of rest to benefit the entire human race.

Lord of the Sabbath

No doubt astounding His detractors, Jesus also referred to Himself as "the Lord of the Sabbath" (see Luke 6:5). For someone who was extremely humble (so humble that He washed His disciples' feet and willingly died the most humiliating death), Yeshua often made seemingly outlandish statements within earshot of those who opposed Him.

Imagine religious people of the day hearing Yeshua claim to be the messianic Son of Man (a reference found in the Book of Daniel), or the Lord of the Sabbath. What was the context?

One Sabbath day, as recorded in Luke chapter 6, Yeshua and His disciples were passing through the fields, when His disciples picked grain and ate it. Some Pharisees standing nearby claimed that the disciples' actions were a form of work, although picking grain and eating it surely did not qualify as labor or service to anyone.

The Pharisees frequently argued with Yeshua, as they were quite possibly members of the same denomination. I'll never forget my surprise the first time an Israeli informed me in a matter-of-fact way that Yeshua was a Pharisee! I had never been taught such things growing up in the Presbyterian Church. But many scholars surmise that Yeshua's family belonged to the prominent sect. (His family would not have belonged to the other main group, the Sadducees, who denied the resurrection.) And so the frequent clashes between Yeshua and His countrymen were not anti-Semitic encounters, but rather "in-house" arguments.

Thinking "outside of the box," Jesus gave the grain watchers a royal answer from the life and times of His ancestor, King David. (I often wonder what thoughts passed through Yeshua's mind concerning His relationship and kinship with David, physically and spiritually.) Reminding His detractors that David appropriated the sacred loaves from the Tabernacle, the Son of David declared boldly, "The Son of Man is Lord even over the Sabbath" (Luke 6:5 NLT). Jesus was referring to the incident in First Samuel 21 in which David ran for his life after learning that King Saul had intended to kill him. David fled to the Tabernacle in Nob, a village in Benjamin, and petitioned the priest Ahimelech for bread. But Ahimelech had nothing to offer except the consecrated bread.

According to Leviticus 24:5-9, this bread before the Presence of the Lord was exceedingly holy and was reserved exclusively for the priesthood. Amazingly, Ahimelech relinquished the consecrated bread for David and his men because they were perceived to be on a holy mission.

The lesson in both incidents is that the spirit of the Law is greater than the letter of the Law. As for Yeshua being the Lord of the Sabbath, if David could eat the blessed bread, how much more should Great David's Greater Son be allowed to heal without condemnation?

Healing on the Sabbath

In the following verse, Luke 6:6, we again find Jesus teaching on another Sabbath in a synagogue. This time a man was present whose right hand was withered with paralysis. In verse 9, Jesus said to those in attendance: "I ask you, which is lawful on the Sabbath day: to do good or to do evil, to save life or to destroy it?" (NCV).

The Scribes and Pharisees kept watching to see if He would actually heal the man, so they could document their accusations of "Sabbath-breaking" against Him. Today, many Jewish people are also watching Jesus, but with far different motives: this time it is not to discover grounds for accusation, but curiosity over whether He is indeed the Messiah for whom they have been waiting!

Many Jews are still faithfully watching for the Messiah. Some, including rabbis, are now intellectually willing to concede that when Messiah comes, He could indeed be Jesus of Nazareth whom Evangelicals believe will make His second appearance! In any case, on that Sabbath day two thousand years ago, Jesus gave the command in the synagogue: "Stretch out your hand!" (Luke 6:10 NASB).

The man's crippled limb was fully restored.

There is a modern-day spiritual application here: among those Jews living in the Diaspora who have forgotten Jerusalem, there are many withered right hands, spiritually speaking. Psalms 137:5 declares: "If I forget you, O Jerusalem, let my right hand wither!" (RSV).

But the Lord of history and the Lord of prophecy is giving the command to stretch their faith, and He is restoring Jewish limbs in the Promised Land before our eyes. The dry bones have reassembled; sinews and flesh now cover them. It is the Lord's doing, and it is marvelous to behold!

More Sabbath Healings

In Luke 13, a woman was healed on the Sabbath:

And He was teaching in one of the synagogues on the Sabbath. And there was a woman who for eighteen years had had a sickness caused by a spirit; and she was bent double, and could not straighten up at all. When Jesus saw her, He called her over and said to her, "Woman, you are freed from your sickness." And He laid His hands on her; and immediately she was made erect again and began glorifying God. But the synagogue official, indignant because Jesus had healed on the Sabbath, began saying to the crowd in response, "There are six days in which work should be done; so come during them and get healed, and not on the Sabbath day." But the Lord answered him and said, "You hypocrites, does not each of you on the Sabbath untie his ox or his donkey from the stall and lead him away to water him? And this woman, a daughter of Abraham as she is, whom Satan has bound for eighteen long years, should she not have been released from this bond on the Sabbath day?" As He said this, all His opponents were being humiliated; and the entire crowd was rejoicing over all the glorious things being done by Him (Luke 13:10-17 NASB).

Think about the agony and drudgery of being bound with a spirit of infirmity for eighteen years. Should this pitiful woman have waited another day for relief? Absolutely not!

The present moment is always the time to be healed. Hebrews 11:1 declares: "Now faith is…." Faith is always *now!* So Yeshua laid His wonderful healing hands upon this daughter of Abraham, and she was instantly straightened. Hallelu-Yah!

I'll never forget, and I will always give glory to the Lord, for enabling me to lay hands on a woman with a similar infirmity, here in Jerusalem on the Street of the Prophets *(Rehov HaNevi'im)*. The woman was a Sephardic Jew, and she welcomed my compassion, kissing my hand after I prayed for her. She was bent over parallel to the pavement. She was straightened and miraculously healed, not instantly, but on a subsequent day when the shadow of my car passed by her again on the Street of the Prophets. As soon as the car shadow fell upon her, she did what she could not do previously: she straightened up and began to run down the street with joy! Hallelu-Yah!

In Luke 14, Jesus healed yet again on the Sabbath:

> *Now it happened, as He went into the house of one of the rulers of the Pharisees to eat bread on the Sabbath, that they watched Him closely. And behold, there was a certain man before Him who had dropsy. And Jesus, answering, spoke to the lawyers and Pharisees, saying, "Is it lawful to heal on the Sabbath?" But they kept silent. And He took him and healed him, and let him go* (Luke 14:1-4 NKJV).

Jesus was having Sabbath lunch in the house of one of the chief Pharisees. In verse 3, He asked a leading question concerning an obvious case for mercy, but they all kept silent, watching to see what He would do.

This time He healed a man plagued by excessive fluid and abnormal swelling. So Jesus relieved the man of his misery and sent him away in peace. His detractors could not reply when Jesus asked pointedly, "Which of you, having a son or an ox that has fallen into a well, will not immediately pull him out on a sabbath day?" (Luke 14:5 RSV). Please note that Jesus clearly likened sickness and disease to a pit! Who falls into a pit and does not want to be rescued? It is surely natural to want to escape from a pit. Do not remain in the pit of sickness and disease without reaching out to the Lord, our Physician. In the Gospels, the Lord is shown to be willing to heal, proving the will of God in the matter. By healing immediately on the Sabbath, Jesus again demonstrated that faith is not something that must wait for another time and another day. In John 5:5-18, Jesus healed a man who had been unable to walk for thirty-eight years. He told the impotent man to "Get up, pick up your pallet and walk" (John 5:8 NASB)—and he did! But in verse 10 we read: "the Jews were saying to the man who was cured, 'It is the Sabbath, and it is not permissible for you to carry your pallet'" (NASB).

When Jesus healed a blind man on the Sabbath, He encountered similar resistance:

> *Therefore some of the Pharisees were saying, "This man is not from God, because He does not keep the Sabbath." But others were saying, "How can a man who is a sinner perform such signs?" And there was a division among them* (John 9:16 NASB).

An Ongoing Issue

The same division goes on today. However, the point I would like to make is that Jesus did not break the Sabbath itself. He broke man-made rules about the Sabbath that effectively prohibited simple acts of mercy.

In modern Israel, healing on the Sabbath goes on in hospitals and in emergency medicine. Today the consensus among the Jewish people is that saving a life takes precedence over Shabbat and *Yom Tov* (Jewish holidays). The edict is this: "The zealous in lifesaving are praiseworthy; those who delay treatment to ask whether it is permitted are spillers of blood."

In summary, Jesus clearly was not a religious legalist. The Son of Man was in love with people, always deeply aware of their individual needs and forever eager to alleviate their suffering and pain. He did not place observance of the Law above the object of the Law, which is love and mercy. The Gospel accounts of the Lord's many acts of healing on the Sabbath assure us that Yeshua is the Great Physician who makes free house calls 24/7. From the Gospels and the Lord's many healings on the Sabbath, we learn that we do not need to wait to be healed as long as we come to Him humbly and ask by faith for His touch.

The Risen Lord reaches through time from the eternal Sabbath and heals us *now* when we put our faith in Him! Remember, He is the same yesterday, today, and forever (see Heb. 13:8).

Expect Him to heal you without delay!

Points to Ponder

1. Setting aside differences as to observances, what is the divine purpose of the Sabbath?

2. What is the real lesson revealed by the experience of David and his men in First Samuel 21, and Jesus and His disciples in Luke 6? How does it affect your views of the Sabbath?

3. When is the perfect time to be healed?

Note

1. "Hebrew Lexicon: H2502 (KJV)," Blue Letter Bible, s.v. "chalats," http://www.blueletterbible.org/lang/lexicon/lexicon.cfm?Strongs=H2502&t=KJV (accessed 24 Oct, 2013).

Chapter 13

BECOMING A HEALER

Proverbs 13:17 says that a "wicked messenger falls into trouble: but a faithful ambassador brings health." Here is how *The Aramaic Bible in Plain English* translates this verse: "An evil messenger falls into affliction and a trustworthy messenger is a healer."[1] Amen!

Ministers are surely healing ambassadors of the Lord because of the high commission we have received to take "saving health" to all nations (see Ps. 67:2). An ambassador is one who accurately comprehends the mind and will of his King. Ambassadors of the Lord accept with great expectation King Messiah's command to accomplish exploits! The Bible abounds with ordinary people accomplishing extraordinary deeds for the kingdom of God.

To begin to pray for the sick, all you have to do is find some willing people who want to get well, and begin to lay your hands upon them, by faith and in the name of Yeshua, Jesus the Messiah!

To demonstrate that it is God's will to heal, and to make provision for our healing, He places within the Body of Messiah people who are especially gifted as miracle-workers and healers. In First Corinthians 12:31, the apostle Paul admonished believers "to earnestly desire" these gifts. Earlier in the chapter he explained: "Now you are the body of Christ, and each one of you is a part of it. And in the church God has appointed first of all apostles, second prophets, third teachers, then *workers of miracles, also those having gifts of healing,* those able to help others, those with gifts of administration, and those speaking in different kinds of tongues" (1 Cor. 12:27-28 NIV).

One of the wonders of endowments distributed by the Holy Spirit is that there is no monopoly on them! And, of course, no one person possesses all the gifts of the Holy Spirit. But everyone does have some type of gift.

Remission of Sins

An important aspect of learning to be a healer is to realize that part of the Great Commission is to remit sins. John 20:23 declares: "Whose soever sins ye remit, they are remitted unto them; and whose soever sins ye retain, they are retained."

This is the work of every believer, not just a priest. True believers are all part of the priesthood of believers: "You also, as living stones, are being built up a spiritual house, a holy priesthood, to offer up spiritual sacrifices acceptable to God through Jesus Christ" (1 Pet. 2:5 NKJV).

Each one of us has authority imparted from the Master, Yeshua, to pray *with* various people that their sins will be forgiven. This is part of the preparation to receive healing. God is the one who does the forgiving as we declare the Good News of the Gospel.

Healing Our Character "Diseases"

Actually, to achieve great things for God, we must also be healed of character diseases. The far-reaching impact of childhood on adult life demands that children be treated wisely by parents. I heard about a family that had five daughters, and when a sixth baby girl was born, she was not cuddled by her parents because they had tried one more time for a boy, and felt they had failed. On the other hand, I also heard about a family where a daughter who was the sixth child after five boys, was spoiled rotten. There is no substitute for godly behavior and character in our homes! Whatever our history, we cannot afford to remain as spiritual babies in some aspects of our personality. Although God can heal people who petition Him in a general way, He prefers to heal people who bring their expressed needs to Him as children talking to their loving parent.

Ask God the Holy Spirit to heal the hurts, rejections, and insults that occurred in your childhood and also in your adulthood—events that have been buried and may still be festering inside of you.

Truly the most therapeutic advice is: "Get over it!" There is no time to stay injured, as it were, incapacitated by the side of the Jericho Road, waiting for the luxury of a priest or the Good Samaritan to pour oil and wine into your wounds. Pick yourself up! Physician, heal thyself!

One way to get over hurts and disappointments is to learn to give thanks to God *in* all things (see 1 Thess. 5:18). Say to the Lord, "I believe You knew that this event, hurt, (whatever, just fill in the blank) would happen to me. I confess that You are well able to bring good, even out of a tragedy."

When you have been belittled or rejected, talk it over with God and say, "Lord, I've been rejected by this person. I acknowledge my hurt; but I refuse to bury pain inside of me. I present this hurt to You to be healed. *Lord, I want to return to normal as quickly as possible.* Take the pain away and give me the power to forgive and forget!"

Now have the faith to thank the Lord for the incident. Why? This is part of growing up. Sometimes hurts and rejections are permitted by God for self to be decentralized and strength of character to be formed. Rejection can also be a practical form of guidance! When we are rejected, a door is closed, and we can move on to where we are appreciated.

Sometimes we need to repent because our self-life is too dominant. When we are not dead to self by reckoning ourselves crucified by faith with Christ, our feelings are often hurt.

Another of the character diseases we can suffer is blaming God and ascribing wrongdoing to the Almighty. This is a serious issue. Although Satan afflicted Job with many sorrows and calamities, Job 1:22 testifies that Job did not "charge God foolishly" with misdeeds.

How many times have we foolishly become angry at God although He is just and holy? This point was made earlier, but bears repeating: instead of murmuring against Him when things go wrong, we need to recognize the more likely root of the problem: rebellious sin or satanic opposition.

The Lord was not overtaken with such character "diseases." He possessed perfect inner peace and self-dominion. Jesus never defended or advertised Himself. He blessed those who cursed Him. He is our best example of a perfectly integrated, whole personality. We can yield to His mindset as He lives through us! (See First Corinthians 2:16.)

Pray that any aspect of your personality that was previously stunted or crippled will begin to grow rapidly. Ask the Lord to help you catch up so your character and personality can be integrated into a beautiful whole with no fractures. As you minister healing to others, may the Lord bless you with the "perfect peace" of Isaiah 26:3 (which in Hebrew is *shalom shalom,* or double peace). Remember that practicing the presence of God must be our constant mindset. Because of His presence and His giftings, we can complete the work we are commissioned as believers to do.

The Gift of Touch

Touch is another aspect of the healing ministry. Somebody with an authentic gift of faith and healing will not be afraid to touch people, and will not be afraid of germs and diseases. This truth had to be settled in my own heart: one of my first ministry assignments in Africa was to minister in a leper colony. I was completely thrilled when a blind leper was healed that day after the laying on of hands!

There is a popular TV show about a detective named Mr. Monk, a character with Obsessive Compulsive Disorder. In many amusing scenes, he wipes his hands with a moist tissue after shaking hands with someone. His idiosyncrasy, of course, offends the person whose hand he shook. If he were a real person, he would need to be delivered from that malady and become a believer before he could ever pray effectively by laying hands on the sick! Jesus had the gift of touch. He touched lepers, healed them, and later became a curse in His own body by absorbing all the curses of sin and sickness of mankind.

Galatians 3:13 teaches us that our Messiah has redeemed us from the curse of the Law. On the Cross, Jesus became, as it were, a spiritual leper; even the ancient rabbis acknowledge that aspect of the Suffering Servant prophecies. Jesus, Yeshua, became a substitutionary curse for us, because it is written: "Cursed is everyone who hangs on a tree" (Gal. 3:13 NKJV; see also Deut. 21:23).

Untouched by the Curse

When our Lord hung on the execution stake of the Cross as the Lamb of God, all of the curses of the Law were laid upon His body. Although He never sinned, He literally became a curse and a sin offering for us. In this divine exchange, we became the righteousness of God. Therefore born-again, blood-washed believers cannot be cursed. Our Lord the Lamb bore all the curses for us! What a complete Savior!

One of my favorite verses is one already mentioned: Proverbs 26:2 says, "...the curse causeless shall not come." When we walk in a holy manner before God, not giving place to the enemy, not allowing our tongues to run riot, a curse has no cause to touch us.

I had to learn this because of my ministry in potentially dangerous places. As I travel through the nations, all sorts of curses reside in atmospheres. Satanically inspired people try to curse ministries. Even professing believers in the Church can greatly oppose genuine ministries. If I would believe that their curses or negative prayers had power to penetrate the covering of the blood of Jesus, I could be defeated. But be assured that when we have not given any place to the devil, and when we are carrying out the will of the Father, the name of the Lord is a high tower of safety. He is our shield; and His redeeming blood is impenetrable!

This sense of security is tested often. I was attending a believers' meeting in a hotel ballroom when a woman called me out of the group. She began to prophesy over me according to her understanding and human thinking. (People sometimes think they are prophesying by the Spirit of God, when they are actually prophesying out of their own human spirit.)

This woman had heard that I was ministering in the nations and in some dangerous places, so she began to prophesy out of her natural fears that terrible curses were being hurled at my ministry. The negative words she "prophesied" became more awful by the moment. If I had received them, I would have become weighed down and oppressed.

The leader of the meeting apparently did not discern that the prophecy was proceeding from a human spirit rather than the Holy Spirit, nor was there any declaration from the leadership that the Lord has given us authority over demons and curses. While this was going on, I said to myself, "I do not receive this!" I maintained my inner peace. Indeed, the Word of God assures us "the curse undeserved cannot alight."

When we know the Word, we can have zero fear. But *we must know God and His Word* to do great exploits. Evangelist Reinhard Bonnke, with whom my husband and I traveled for five years, also believes that he cannot be cursed. Once, when he was met at the airport in India, a pastor who greeted him asked, "Pastor Bonnke, do you feel it?" "Feel what?" Reinhard said. "The presence of India's millions of gods!" the pastor answered. "No!" Reinhard said, "I am only aware of the presence of the Holy Spirit!" *That* is the mentality of an overcomer! Always be aware of the presence of the Holy Spirit!

The Restoration of All Things

Acts 3:21 declares that the Lord must remain in heaven until the time of the restoration of all things. Part of that restoration is the Gospel of healing.

Perseverance is required to move from failure to success in the healing ministry. Smith Wigglesworth, the great "apostle of faith" of the last century, once advised that if the person you are praying for dies, your response should be to step over him and pray for the next person!

Yes, indeed, we have to persevere to recover the healing message! One of the signs of the Second Coming is the outpouring of the Holy Spirit on all flesh and the restoration of the gifts of the Spirit, including the gift of faith and the gifts of healings. As I have already stated, a time of restoration even greater than the Early Church is anticipated by many. I, however, am personally challenged by the Lord's piercing, prophetic question: "When the Son of Man comes, will He find faith on the earth?" (Luke 18:8 NASB).

Just as the occult increases to counterfeit the gifts of the Spirit, so the anointing of the Holy Spirit should be greater upon the Bride of Christ. Without spot or blemish, may we have a sickless testimony to the greater works of Jesus our Messiah, the Anointed One. Doubt and unbelief are more dangerous now because of the large accumulation of miracle testimonies in our time (by God's grace and mercy to our generation). In John 14:12, Yeshua said His followers would do His works and even "greater works" because He was going to the Father, to send us the power of the Holy Spirit. Yet, even with more miracles occurring, faith is not increasing.

Have you cleansed any lepers lately? Have you raised the dead lately? I am not being glib. I am encouraging you to get started doing the first works of Jesus! When you are comfortable doing the New Testament miracles of Jesus, then you can move on to accomplish the inexhaustible "greater works" that He prophesied for all who believe!

The Expanding Circle of Faith

The classic definition of faith was given in Hebrews 11:1: "Now faith is the substance of things hoped for, the evidence of things not seen." A lot of people are not able to grasp that Bible definition. But there is another way of explaining faith. It can be compared to comfort zones or circles. There may be a certain level up to which you can comfortably believe God and stay in faith, but there is a point where you can no longer comfortably believe Him. At that point, you are outside your current level, or circle of faith. Growing in faith is like moving from one comfort zone to the next. For example, you may be comfortable believing God to heal a headache. But perhaps you cannot believe God to heal diseases or cancer. Believing that is outside your comfort zone; you are then uncomfortable and prone to doubt.

.ever one day, as you grow in faith, meditate on God's Word, .ctice praying for the sick, and begin to see some results, you suddenly perceive that you are comfortable with believing God to heal cancer! Congratulations! Your circle of faith limitation has been enlarged and you have moved from one comfort zone to another. You discover the ever-increasing circle of faith where you are comfortable and able to believe.

However, you might still hesitate to believe God when it comes to healing people in wheelchairs. After a period of growth, and continuing to pray faithfully for the needs of people, you wake up to the realization that you *can* believe God to heal people in wheelchairs! So you pray for somebody in a wheelchair and the person is healed! The next time, you are more comfortable praying for people in wheelchairs, because your faith has been stretched to another comfort zone where you are no longer intimidated.

And so the circle expands, until, one day, you can believe to raise somebody from the dead! This ongoing process is part of the law of progression: we move from faith to faith, from strength to strength, from victory to victory, and from glory to glory.

Where Do I Start?

You cannot start at the top rung of a ladder. Faith is stretched, and it grows. In order for you to participate in this last great wave of healing restoration, you need to start exercising your faith now. Read all the scriptures on healing in both the Old and New Covenants. Meditate on these healing promises.

Faith is action. So begin to act on the Word of God. Speak to mountains to be moved!

Practice the command of Jesus to lay hands on the sick by praying for your close family members. If you are a parent, lay hands on your children when they feel poorly. If you are a child, lay hands on your brothers and sisters or on your parents if they fall sick.

Keep a bottle of consecrated anointing oil in your home to use when you pray for one another's needs. As you act in faith, you will begin to see results. If you do not see immediate results, do not give up. Results come through patience and the spiritual law of use. It is as Jesus taught: to those who have, more will be given (see Matt. 13:12).

Healing by Proxy

Concerning healing by proxy from a distance, it is our privilege to pray for people to be healed either "up close and personal" or from a distance. Jesus taught us by example to cast out demons and to pray for the sick either through the laying on of hands, anointing with oil, or speaking the word of deliverance from any distance.

In Matthew 8, a Roman centurion approached Jesus to heal his servant. Jesus was no respecter of rank or position; He healed both noblemen and servants alike. Jesus immediately agreed to go to the centurion's house. Not wishing to burden Rabbi Jesus with issues concerning visiting a Gentile's house, the centurion made a practical suggestion: all Jesus had to do was to "speak the word" of healing!

Jesus marveled at the centurion's great faith. And it was reported that the centurion's servant was healed at that very hour. There was no physical contact, *only faith*.

In Matthew 15:22, a Canaanite woman approached Jesus crying, "Lord, Son of David, have mercy on me! My daughter is suffering terribly from demon-possession" (NIV).

To test her faith, the Lord replied, "It is not right to take the children's bread and toss it to their dogs" (Matt. 15:26 NIV).

The woman responded with determination:

> *"Yes, Lord," she said, "but even the dogs eat the crumbs that fall from their masters' table." Then Jesus answered, "Woman, you have great faith! Your request is granted." And her daughter was healed from that very hour* (Matthew 15:27-28 NIV).

Because of these verses you can be assured of a potential worldwide ministry without ever leaving your house. Healing can be accomplished through conversations, letters, telephone calls, and the Internet.

A woman asked me to pray for her brother who was suffering agonizing pain caused by sciatica. He was unable to walk a few steps, and he could not sleep. Via email, she explained: "He can't stand or do even a simple task like cutting an orange."

I replied, "I rebuke this pain and sickness in the name of Jesus! When the Lord spoke the Word, people were healed, so I do the same. We must believe that God honors our faith at all times. Say 'Amen'! I'm in faith that you will send me a good report!"

The woman replied, "Thank You, Jesus!" and went on to explain: "The Lord has answered your prayer! This morning my brother got out of bed and walked for the first time in weeks without a stick. No pain!"

Truly, there is no distance in God when we pray! In Him we live and move and have our being (see Acts 17:28).

Many Gifts, One Body

Concerning healing, there are as many gifts in the Body of Messiah as there are diseases! In fact, God most certainly has more gifts than the devil has diseases!

These gifts are distributed, as Scripture reveals: "to another faith by the same Spirit; to another the gifts of healing by the same Spirit..." (1 Cor. 12:9). In this verse the word for gifts is *charismata,* which is plural. The gifts of healings are the supernatural abilities given to manifold members of the Body to cure myriad maladies.

Because various gifts are distributed as the Holy Spirit wills, some believers are more gifted than others to heal certain sicknesses. Some healers possess particular gifts to heal bad backs, barrenness, cancer, blindness, or deafness, etc., but they may not have equal faith for other maladies. Other members of the Body of Messiah will be gifted for faith to heal a variety of other infirmities and diseases, just as there are specialists in medicine. Everybody has a piece of the puzzle, so to speak. We have need of one another!

In Conclusion

You will never learn about healing in any real way until you stop merely observing others and begin, by faith, to act yourself. I devoured lots of books by well-known Evangelical healers before I began to step out to pray for the sick. Just watching Reinhard Bonnke and other mentors in action was greatly edifying and better than reading ten books.

I praise God for these anointed ministries, but one act of faith on my part to pray for the sick was more beneficial to my faith growth. Why? Because when you begin to move out in faith, obeying the promptings of the Holy Spirit, your teacher becomes the Holy Spirit Himself!

When you move in faith, you have the attention and help of the original Teacher, not a well-known author or mentor. You begin to build up, not book knowledge, but your own experiences—real-life victories and practical knowledge.

Jesus is alive and still works amazing miracles today. He wants to do them through you! He wants to move mountains through you!

Points to Ponder

1. Have you specifically asked God to reveal and heal the hurts, rejections, and insults that have touched your life? What does your answer reveal about your willingness to approach Him with childlike faith?

2. Do fears about potential dangers in ministry keep you from stepping forward in your calling? How so, and how might your mindset change for the better?

3. Consider your personal circle of faith. What are some earmarks of its continued expansion?

Note

1. The Original Aramaic New Testament in Plain English with Psalms & Proverbs, 5th edition, BibleHub.com, (2010), http://biblehub.com/aramaic-plain-english/proverbs/13.htm (accessed October 25, 2013).

Appendix

SALVATION AND HEALING PRAYER

This book has come into your hands with my love and hope for your health and well-being. I encourage you to open your heart to the Lord and ask Him to forgive you of all known and unknown sins, to save your soul and to heal your body. For an assurance in your heart concerning both salvation and healing, I invite you to say out loud the following statement as both a prayer and faith declaration:

> *Thank You, Father God, that Jesus fully paid the penalty at the Cross for the forgiveness of all my sins and for the healing of all my sickness, infirmity, pain, and disease. I believe He was raised from the dead, and I confess with my mouth that Jesus is Lord. Your Word promises that all who call upon the name of the Lord shall be saved. Therefore, I call upon Jesus (Yeshua the Messiah) and I am saved, spirit, soul, and body! I do believe Your Word that "Surely He has born my sickness and carried my pains, and He was wounded for my transgressions. He was bruised for my iniquities. The chastisement for my peace was upon Him, and by His stripes, I was healed!" Amen and amen!*

Dear friend, if this book has strengthened your faith, and if you have been healed as a result of reading this book, please contact me at www.exploits.tv so that we can rejoice together!

ABOUT THE AUTHOR

Christine Darg has been privileged to minister on every habitable continent and in the most far-flung islands. Her *Exploits Ministry* is based upon Daniel 11:32 and John 14:12. She is obeying the Great Commission to fulfill the mandate of Acts 1:8 to the ends of the earth.

Christine is the author of many books, including *The Wounded Lover, Miracles Among Muslims, The Spirit of Excellence,* and *Let Ishmael Live!* Her TV programs are broadcast 24/7 worldwide at www.jerusalemchannel.tv.

Christine has learned much about spiritual warfare and healing. One of her earliest childhood memories is an open vision in which Jesus appeared at the side of her crib, and healed her of a life-threatening illness. When she was sixteen, she was seated in a car that was hit by a train. Her life was miraculously saved as a ministering angel tended to her at the accident scene. The Lord said, "I have spared your life for a purpose!" A third attempt on her life by a serious, near-death emergency occurred before Christine and her family moved to Jerusalem to begin strategic television work for *The 700 Club.* She has learned to fight the fight of faith and encourages others to do so!

Along with her husband Peter, Christine traveled extensively with evangelist Reinhard Bonnke in Africa for five years to document the preaching of God's Word with miraculous signs and wonders. She witnessed the deaf hearing, the blind seeing, and the lame walking.

Subsequently, Christine has held her own large Gospel campaigns in Eastern Europe, the Philippines, the Middle East, Africa, Pakistan, and India, with testimonies of many salvations and healings to the glory of

God. She has seen blind eyes opened in a leprosy colony in Nigeria. People have abandoned wheelchairs. Sufferers have been healed of debilitating diseases. Tumors have vanished. Crippled limbs and spines have been restored—all to the glory of the Lord our Healer.

To contact Christine, to join the Every Friday Fast to set spiritual captives free, or to receive *Exploits Ministry* updates, visit her website at www.exploits.tv.

You can also correspond with the author at the following addresses:

PO Box 14085 Jaffa Gate, East Jerusalem 91140 Israel

PO Box 109 Hereford, England, HR4 9XR

PO Box 71780 Henrico, VA 23255-1780 USA

Another exciting book from
Christine Darg

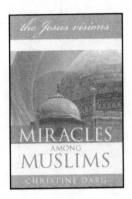

MIRACLES AMONG MUSLIMS *The Jesus Visions*

Christine Darg heard the voice of God in a dream say, "Go!" to an Arabian city where the Holy Spirit was moving in Revival. She chronicles outstanding dreams and visions in this current move of God, and also shares some of the startling visions she herself has experienced in the Middle East and throughout the world.

The Jesus Visions is an amazing account of signs and wonders in the Muslim world because Jesus continues to be the same yesterday, today and forever! For many centuries of desert-like dryness in the Middle East, the word of the LORD was precious. There was no open vision. But suddenly, in the fullness of time, the spiritual scenario in the Middle East has changed. God is pouring out His Spirit in the dry places before the LORD's return.

Order now from Evangelista Media
Telephone: +39 085 959806 - Fax: +39 085 9090113
E-mail: orders@evangelistamedia.com

Internet: www.evangelistamedia.com

Additional copies of this book and other book
titles from EVANGELISTA MEDIA™
and DESTINY IMAGE™ EUROPE
are available at your local bookstore.

We are adding new titles every month!

To view our complete catalog online, visit us at:
www.evangelistamedia.com

Follow us on Facebook
(facebook.com/EvangelistaMedia)
and Twitter (twitter.com/EM_worldwide)

Send a request for a catalog to:

Via Maiella, 1
66020 San Giovanni Teatino (Ch), ITALY
Tel. +39 085 959806 • Fax +39 085 9090113
info@evangelistamedia.com

"Changing the World, One Book at a Time."

Are you an author?
Do you have a "today" God-given message?

CONTACT US

We will be happy to review your manuscript
for the possibility of publication:

publisher@evangelistamedia.com
http://www.evangelistamedia.com/pages/AuthorsAppForm.htm

DATE DUE